CLASSIC COOKIES

166 Favorite Recipes to Enjoy ALL YEAR

FOX CHAPEL
PUBLISHING

CLASSIC COOKIES

166 Favorite Recipes
to Enjoy
ALL YEAR

Includes Cookies, Bars, and a
Special Holiday Season Selection

By Kate Woodson

ISBN 978-1-4971-0388-7

Library of Congress Control Number: 2023942306

Recipe selection, design, and book design © Fox Chapel Publishing. Recipes and photographs © G&R Publishing DBA CQ Products, unless otherwise noted.

Shutterstock images: AtlasStudio (front cover, top); ; Ipich (back cover, illustration; interior striped illustrations); VectoRay (serving size illustration); Kwitka (101, 113, 121, 125, 133, 137, arrows); wavebreakmedia (10); Charles Brutlag (11, top; 140, bottom); photosarahjackson (35); Matt Gibson (56); Martin Gardeazabal (57); iLight photo (72, top); P Maxwell Photography (72, bottom); Radu Bercan (73, top); Redha Ali (73, bottom); Marie Rosemary (74, top); ArchMarwa (74, bottom); Vladislav Noseek (75); Smelenna (76, top); Yulia Gladysheva (76, bottom); Muhammad Senopati (77); Photon Collective (78, top); Carolina Arroyo (78, bottom); Alexandria Hill (79); ianmitchinson (138, top); Sawable (139); Brent Hofacker (140, bottom; 146, top); Candice Bell (141); istetiana (142, top); Barnaby Staniland (142, bottom); Lando Aviles (143, top); Nataliya Arzamasova (143, bottom); DronG (144, bottom; 145); Alp Galip (146, bottom); Joanna 12 (147); Bandy (148, top); NoirChocolate (148, bottom); Erhan Inga (149, top); from my point of view (149, bottom); Bartosz Luczak (158, bottom); Marie C Fields, (173); Elena Veselova (180, top); Carolyn Dietrich (181).

To learn more about the other great books from Fox Chapel Publishing, or to find a retailer near you, call toll-free 800-457-9112 or visit us at www.FoxChapelPublishing.com.

We are always looking for talented authors. To submit an idea, please send a brief inquiry to acquisitions@foxchapelpublishing.com.

Printed in China
First printing

Table of Contents

21

36

52

64

78

92

98

105

118

122

133

145

154

162

170

Making cookies with loved ones, like at Christmastime here, creates memories and traditions that will stay with you long after the timer goes off.

Introduction

What do Christmas Eve, bake sales, dinner parties, and cozy nights in all have in common? They're occasions that are made better by a warm, delicious cookie, of course! Gooey, soft, chewy, crunchy, crispy, and more, cookies have a variety of textures, shapes, sizes, and flavors to satisfy every sweet craving and snack time. Some people prefer chocolate chip while others love snickerdoodles, cinnamon raisin, peanut butter, white chocolate macadamia, and loads more. In this book, I'll show you how to make traditional favorites along with cookie bars, holiday cookies, and even no-bake and gluten-free options. Cookies are my favorite dessert to make—not only is the baking simple, with hardly any preparation required, but the act of making cookies brings people together. Grab the ingredients, tools, and the people you love, and within minutes you will have not only delicious cookies to show for it, but countless memories to relive with each bite you take for years to come. Within the next pages, you will find helpful information to ensure you make the perfect cookies each time. So, whether you're interested in bringing a traditional favorite to your next holiday event, or creating a new classic for your loved ones, I'm sure you'll find the perfect treat in this book. Let's get baking!

-Kate

I make these Pumpkin Cheesecake Doodles (page 178) every year for Thanksgiving dessert. It's one of my family's favorite treats!

Although prep time is minimal, it's important to make sure you have the tools you need before you start, like mixing bowls, measuring cups, spatulas, cooling racks, and more.

What You'll Need

- Baking sheets and pans. For cookie bars, the baking pan size is listed for each recipe.

- Measuring cups

- Spatula and/or whisk

- Mixing bowls. Powered mixers can also be used.

- Parchment paper (optional but recommended)

- Cooling rack

- Other tools are listed in each recipe description.

Techniques

Most people have experienced a cookie mishap, like flat cookies, hard cookies, burnt cookies, undercooked cookies, and anything else you can imagine. Don't let this intimidate you! These tips and tricks will guide you to cookie perfection.

- Use all-purpose white flour and granulated white sugar unless otherwise specified by the recipe. Spoon the flour, sugar, and other dry ingredients into your measuring cups (separately), then level off with a flat edge.

Always pack brown sugar—it should hold the cup's shape.

- Check liquid measurements at eye level, and let dairy products warm up to room temperature before using.

- Use eggs at room temperature. In a hurry? Put eggs in a bowl with lukewarm water until they reach room temperature. Avoid overbeating eggs; this leads to flat cookies.

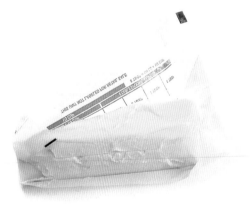

- It's best to use unsalted butter unless otherwise specified by the recipe. To soften butter, let stand at room temperature a few hours, or microwave in 10- to 15-second increments until mushy or melted (depending on what the recipe calls for). Try to avoid margarine.

- Use the right leavening—baking soda and baking powder aren't interchangeable. And don't omit salt—it balances the flavors.

- Chilling the cookie dough helps to prevent the cookies from flattening in the oven. Putting dough in the fridge for 10–20 minutes after mixing will help harden the dough before baking.

- Line or grease your sheets and pans!

- For baking sheets, parchment paper is the best lining technique. Nonstick silicone baking mats are also a great lining option. If you don't have parchment paper or a baking mat, there's no need to grease your baking sheet, since most sheets are nonstick and cookies will be slick enough to remove. Note that a bare baking sheet may lead to crispier cookie bottoms.

- For baking pans, parchment paper is also the best option for lining. You can fold/cut the corners of the paper to fit the pan's shape. Foil can also be used, but it will need to be sprayed with nonstick spray. Butter is a great greasing option for your pan if lining isn't available; just use a stick of

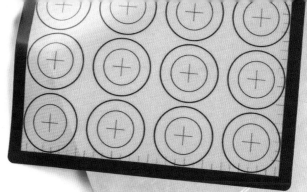

butter to wipe against the bottom and sides of the pan!

- The serving sizes are listed for each recipe. However, the number of cookies you make is ultimately up to you! Big or small, the cookies will always be delicious.

- When cookies are finished, let them sit and cool for a few minutes (or for as long as the recipe specifies) until you're able to transfer them to a cooling rack. You can eat them fresh out of the oven or let them cool for as long as you want. Note that leaving them on the hot baking sheet for too long may result in overcooked cookies, or will make them stick to the baking sheet.

Let your cookies cool on a cooling rack before eating . . . even though it's tempting to dig right in!

- You can bake all the dough in one day and save extra cookies in a sealed container, or make a few small servings at a time and store your cookie dough in the fridge. For food safety, raw dough should only be refrigerated for two to four days. Otherwise, freeze your dough for up to two months.

- Cleaning your baking sheet or pan is simple! Rinse or soak your sheets with warm, soapy water, and gently scrub any residue with a sponge.

CHILL OUT!

Chilling dough in the fridge helps cookies develop more flavor and keep their shape during baking. If you're in a hurry, quick-chill dough in the freezer for one-third or the time. For fresh-baked drop cookies anytime, freeze cookie-size scoops of dough until firm, then toss them into a container and keep frozen until a craving hits. Thaw slightly and bake as directed.

What's more fun than a cookie? A cookie bar. All the flavor, half the effort!

Cookie Bars

Cookie bars have all the deliciousness of cookies, but are just pressed into a pan. No scooping and rolling, no waiting for the pan to cook between batches, and the best part is that you can still have that classic chocolate chip or snickerdoodle taste! If you're in a hurry, yummy no-bake recipes are an option too. Just mix, press, and eat. Here are a few extra tips to get you started with cookie bar magic:

- All ingredients and pan prep for cookies seamlessly apply to cookie bars as well.

- When cookie bars are finished, grab the ends of the lining and transfer to a cutting board. Use a chef's knife to cut the sheet of baked cookie bar into squares. If there's no lining, cut the cookie bar in the pan with a soft, non-metal knife or spatula.

Pan Size	Servings	Approx. Bar Size
8" x 8"	16	2" x 2" (4 rows x 4 rows)
9" x 9"	25	1 ¾" x 1 ¾" (5 rows x 5 rows)
7" x 11"	24	1 ¾" x 1 ¾" (4 rows x 6 rows)
9" x 13"	36	2 ¼" x 1 ½" (4 rows x 9 rows)
11" x 15"	54	1 ¾" x 1 ⅔" (6 rows x 9 rows)
12" x 18"	72	1 ½" x 2" (8 rows x 9 rows)

- What's the serving size? The number of squares you cut is ultimately up to you! However, you can use this size chart to determine the serving size for each pan.

Allergy Substitutions

If you're gluten free, dairy free, nut free, or if you just like to avoid these ingredients in your diet, have no fear! You can make easy substitutions in each cookie recipe. Also, in this book there are multiple gluten-free recipes already made that are labeled with a gluten-free symbol to help you locate a safe cookie if you have an allergy. Here are some substitutions for you to keep in mind.

- If you're gluten free, you can substitute gluten-free all-purpose flour for normal white flour. The brand you choose is up to you but be sure to check the measurement conversion directions on the package. Gluten-free flours must contain xanthan gum for the proper texture. If your flour doesn't have xanthan gum, you will need to add it separately.

- Dairy-free butter can be substituted for regular butter.

- Be aware there are multiple recipes in this book that contain nuts. Nuts can be removed from some recipes, but not all nut recipes are able to be altered.

- Dairy-free milk like oat milk and almond milk can be substituted for normal dairy milk.

Some cookies in this book, like the Monster Cookie Bars (on page 92), are already made with gluten-free ingredients, but with substitutions, you can amend any recipe to fit your diet!

Traditional Cookies

The cookies in this section are the cookies that you most likely know and love. Oatmeal, chocolate chips, M&Ms, peanut butter, and so many more sweet treats are packed into these cookies. However, you might be pleasantly surprised at the other ingredients that turn a traditional round cookie into something sweet, unique, and utterly addictive.

Betwixed

MAKES 3 ½ DOZEN

Ingredients

- 1 ½ cups butter, softened
- 1 cup powdered sugar
- 1 teaspoon vanilla
- 3 cups flour
- ¼ teaspoon salt
- 50 caramels, unwrapped, about 1 (11-ounce) bag
- 1 tablespoon water
- 1 (11 ½-ounce) package milk chocolate chips
- 2 teaspoons shortening

1. Preheat the oven to 350°F and line cookie sheets with parchment paper; set aside.

2. In a medium mixing bowl, beat the butter and powdered sugar until smooth and creamy. Mix in the vanilla, flour, and salt until well blended.

3. Shape dough into two disks and roll out on a lightly floured surface until ½" thick.

4. Cut into rounds with a 2-inch cookie cutter and arrange on prepped cookie sheets, rerolling the scraps to cut more rounds.

5. Bake 14 to 16 minutes or until just beginning to brown. Let cool.

6. In a large microwaveable bowl, combine caramels and water. Microwave on high for 2 to 2 ½ minutes, stirring every minute until smooth.

7. Spread caramel on each cookie, reheating caramel as needed. Let these beauties cool.

8. Combine the chocolate chips and shortening in another microwaveable bowl and microwave on high for 30 seconds at a time, stirring until melted.

9. Spread chocolate over the cooled caramel and let stand until set.

10. Store at room temperature. Freezing not recommended. Enjoy!

When is a Twix candy bar NOT a candy bar? When it's turned into a caramel-topped, chocolate-kissed shortbread cookie. Brilliant.

Cinnamon Roll Cookies

MAKES 2½ DOZEN

Ingredients

- 1 cup plus 6 tablespoons unsalted butter, softened
- ⅓ cup sugar
- 1 cup powdered sugar, divided
- 1 teaspoon salt, divided
- 2 ½ teaspoons vanilla, divided
- 1 ½ teaspoons orange zest
- 1 egg
- 2 cups plus 2 tablespoons flour, divided
- ¼ cup light brown sugar
- 1 ½ teaspoons plus 2 tablespoons light corn syrup, divided
- 1 tablespoon cinnamon
- Water, as needed

1. In a large mixing bowl, beat together 1 cup butter, the sugar, ¾ cup powdered sugar, ½ teaspoon salt, 1 teaspoon vanilla, and zest on medium speed until light and fluffy, 3 to 4 minutes.

2. Add the egg and beat well. Slowly beat in 2 cups flour until just combined.

3. Roll out the dough on a lightly floured surface to make a 12-inch square. (A silicone mat or parchment paper works great for this dough.)

4. For the filling, beat together the brown sugar, 1 ½ teaspoons corn syrup, cinnamon, ½ teaspoon vanilla, and the remaining 6 tablespoons butter, ½ teaspoon salt, and 2 tablespoons flour on medium speed for 2 to 3 minutes, until light and fluffy.

5. Spread this cinnamon confection over the dough.

6. Starting at one edge, roll dough into a log shape. Wrap in plastic wrap, pressing gently to make roll even. Freeze at least 20 minutes, until firm (or refrigerate overnight).

7. To bake the cookies, preheat the oven to 375°F and line cookie sheets with parchment paper. Unwrap the dough log and cut into slices, ⅜ inch thick. Arrange on prepped cookie sheets and bake 12 to 14 minutes or until edges are slightly browned.

8. Let cookies cool a few minutes before removing to a wire rack to finish cooling.

9. For the glaze, whisk together the remaining ¼ cup powdered sugar, 1 teaspoon vanilla, and 2 tablespoons corn syrup until smooth, adding up to 1 tablespoon water as needed to make a thin glaze.

10. Brush the glaze over each cookie and let dry. (These freeze best without the glaze.) Serve and enjoy!

Almost like eating a
cinnamon roll—but
this one's crisp and
crunchy. Delish!

Nutty Fruit Clusters

MAKES
2
DOZEN

Ingredients

- 1 (12-ounce) package white baking chips
- 1 cup dried fruit, such as cranberries, raisins, diced apricots, etc.
- 2 cups Chex cereal
- ¼ cup peanuts

1. In a large microwave-safe bowl, heat white chocolate chips in microwave, stopping to stir every 30 seconds, until completely melted.
2. Gently stir in fruit, Chex cereal, and peanuts. Mix until well coated.
3. Drop by tablespoonfuls onto waxed paper. Refrigerate for 1 hour.
4. Cover and store in refrigerator until serving. Enjoy!

Chocolatey Cereal Bites

MAKES
4
DOZEN

Ingredients

- 24 ounces almond bark
- 2 cups Honey Nut Cheerios cereal
- 2 cups Rice Krispies cereal
- 2 cups peanuts, chopped

1. In a microwave-safe bowl, melt almond bark on high, about 2 to 3 minutes, until soft and creamy.
2. Add the Honey Nut Cheerios, Rice Krispies, and peanuts. Stir until completely mixed.
3. Drop by teaspoonfuls onto waxed paper. Cookies will firm as they cool. Enjoy!

Peanutty Chocolate Chippers

MAKES 5 DOZEN

Ingredients

- ½ cup butter, softened
- ½ cup shortening
- ½ cup peanut butter
- ½ cup sugar
- 1 cup light brown sugar

- 1 teaspoon baking soda
- 2 eggs
- 1 teaspoon vanilla
- 3 cups flour
- ½ cup semi-sweet chocolate chips

- ½ cup milk chocolate chips
- ½ cup honey roasted peanuts, chopped
- ½ cup bite-size peanut butter cups, halved

1. Preheat the oven to 350°F. In a big mixing bowl, beat together the softened butter, shortening, and peanut butter on medium speed about 30 seconds.

2. Add the sugar, light brown sugar, and baking soda and beat until well combined. Beat in eggs and vanilla until blended.

3. Slowly beat in flour, stirring in the rest with a spoon when dough seems stiff.

4. Stir in the semi-sweet and milk chocolate chips, chopped honey roasted peanuts, and bite-size peanut butter cups (halved).

5. Drop the dough by rounded teaspoonful, 2 inches apart, onto parchment paper-lined cookie sheets and bake 11 to 14 minutes or until light golden brown.

6. Cool slightly, then remove to a wire rack to cool completely. (These freeze well.) Serve and enjoy!

Oatmeal Spice Sandwiches

MAKES
2
DOZEN

Ingredients

- 3 cups quick oats, coarsely ground
- 1 ½ cups flour
- 1 teaspoon baking soda
- ½ teaspoon salt
- ¾ teaspoon cinnamon
- ¼ teaspoon ground cloves
- 1 ¾ cups unsalted butter, softened and divided

- ½ cup sugar
- 1 cup dark brown sugar
- 1 egg
- 1 tablespoon molasses
- 2 ½ teaspoons vanilla, divided
- 1 (7-ounce) tub marshmallow crème
- 1 cup powdered sugar
- 1 (13-ounce) jar Nutella hazelnut spread

1. Preheat the oven to 375°F and line cookie sheets with parchment paper. In a bowl, mix the oats, flour, baking soda, ½ teaspoon salt, cinnamon, and cloves and set aside.

2. In a mixing bowl, beat 1 ¼ cups butter, sugar, and brown sugar on medium speed until light and creamy. Beat in egg, molasses, and 2 teaspoons vanilla until blended.

3. Slowly beat in the set-aside oats mixture, stirring in any remainder with a spoon.

4. Drop dough by large spoonfuls (2 tablespoons per cookie) onto prepped cookie sheets, 2 inches apart.

5. Flatten tops lightly and bake 9 to 12 minutes or until edges are lightly browned.

6. Cool slightly, then remove to a wire rack to finish cooling.

7. For the filling, beat the remaining ½ cup butter on high speed until creamy; beat in marshmallow crème. Slowly beat in the powdered sugar and remaining ½ teaspoon vanilla until fluffy.

8. Spread some filling on the bottom of half the cookies and Nutella on the bottom of remaining cookies. Sandwich cookies together, filling sides in. (Freezing not recommended.) Serve and enjoy!

Double the fun when a marshmallow crème filling and Nutella are sandwiched between two yummy oatmeal cookies.

Chocolate Rolo Rounds

MAKES
4
DOZEN

Ingredients

- 2 ¾ cups flour
- ¾ cup unsweetened cocoa powder
- 1 teaspoon baking soda
- ¼ teaspoon salt
- 1 cup butter, softened
- 1 cup sugar
- 1 cup light brown sugar

- 2 eggs
- 2 teaspoons vanilla
- 48 Rolo chocolate-covered caramels, unwrapped
- ½ cup caramel bits
- 1 ½ to 2 tablespoons heavy cream
- Coarse sea salt, for sprinkling

1. Whisk together the flour, cocoa powder, baking soda, and salt in a bowl and set aside.

2. Beat the butter in a large mixing bowl on medium speed until creamy. Add the sugar and brown sugar and beat until well combined. Beat in the eggs and vanilla, then gradually beat in as much of the set-aside flour mixture as possible, stirring in the rest with a spoon. Cover and chill dough about 1 hour.

3. To bake the cookies, preheat the oven to 375°F and line cookie sheets with parchment paper. Shape dough into 1½-inch balls, press a Rolo inside each one, and wrap dough around candy to seal it inside.

4. Set on prepped cookie sheets, 2 inches apart, and bake 8 to 10 minutes or until edges are firm. Cool a few minutes before removing to a wire rack to cool completely.

5. Meanwhile, combine the caramel bits and cream in a microwaveable bowl and microwave on high for 30 to 40 seconds; stir until melted and smooth.

6. Drizzle the caramel over each cookie and sprinkle with sea salt. Let stand until set. (These freeze well.) Serve and enjoy!

Nothing beats melted caramel goodness baked inside a delicious chocolate cookie—until you drizzle more caramel over the top and add a sprinkling of sea salt. Double the bliss!

White Chocolate Macadamia Cookies

MAKES 3 DOZEN

Ingredients

- 2 cups plus 2 tablespoons flour
- ½ teaspoon baking soda
- ¼ teaspoon salt
- ¾ cup unsalted butter, softened
- ½ cup sugar
- 1 cup light brown sugar
- 1 egg plus 1 egg yolk
- 2 teaspoons vanilla
- ¾ cup white chocolate chips
- ¾ cup macadamia nuts, coarsely chopped

1. In a medium bowl, stir together the flour, baking soda, and salt; set aside.

2. In a large mixing bowl, beat the butter, sugar, and brown sugar on medium speed until creamy. Mix in the egg, egg yolk, and vanilla until just combined. Slowly beat in the set-aside flour mixture until well blended.

3. Stir in the chips and nuts; cover and chill the dough at least 1 hour (or up to 5 days).

4. To bake the cookies, preheat the oven to 350°F and line cookie sheets with parchment paper. Drop the dough by rounded tablespoonful onto prepped cookie sheets, about 2 inches apart. (Keep dough refrigerated between batches.)

5. Bake 9 to 12 minutes or until light golden brown. Let cookies cool slightly before removing to a wire rack to cool completely. (These freeze well.) Serve and enjoy!

German Chocolate Drops

MAKES 2 ½ DOZEN

Ingredients

- 1 ¼ cups flour
- ⅓ cup unsweetened cocoa powder
- 1 teaspoon baking powder
- ¼ teaspoon salt
- ¾ cup unsalted butter, softened and divided

- ¾ cup sugar, divided
- ¾ cup dark brown sugar
- 1 egg plus 2 egg yolks, divided
- 1 ½ teaspoon vanilla, divided
- 1 ⅓ cups semi-sweet chocolate chips, divided

- ½ cup evaporated milk
- ½ cup sweetened flaked coconut
- ½ cup chopped pecans

1. Preheat the oven to 350°F and line cookie sheets with parchment paper. In a bowl, whisk together the flour, cocoa powder, baking powder, and salt and set aside.

2. In a mixing bowl, beat ½ cup butter, ¼ cup sugar, and brown sugar on medium-high speed until well mixed. Add the egg, 1 egg yolk, and 1 teaspoon vanilla; beat until combined.

3. Slowly beat in the set-aside flour mixture and then stir in 1 cup chocolate chips.

4. Drop dough by big spoonfuls onto prepped cookie sheets, 2 inches apart, and bake 10 to 12 minutes or until set. Cool slightly, then remove to wire racks until cool.

5. For the toppings, whisk together the milk and remaining ¼ cup butter, ½ cup sugar, and egg yolk in a saucepan over medium heat. Cook and stir often until thickened, about 10 minutes.

6. Remove from heat and stir in coconut, pecans, and remaining ½ teaspoon vanilla; let cool to thicken. Spread mixture on cookies.

7. Melt the remaining ⅓ cup chocolate chips and drizzle over cookies. Let cool at least 15 minutes. (Freezing not recommended.) Serve and enjoy!

Coconut-pecan creaminess perched on a crisp double-chocolate cookie: heaven!

Grandma's Date and Raisin Cookies

MAKES
4
DOZEN

Ingredients

- ⅔ cup butter, softened
- 1⅓ cups plus ½ cup sugar, divided
- ¾ teaspoon vanilla
- 2 eggs
- 2⅔ cups flour

- ¼ teaspoon salt
- 1½ teaspoons cornstarch
- ¼ teaspoon cinnamon
- 1 cup chopped dates
- ½ cup raisins

- ½ cup water
- ½ teaspoon orange extract
- ½ teaspoon orange zest
- ½ cup powdered sugar
- 2–3 teaspoons milk

1. In a large mixing bowl, beat together the butter and 1⅓ cups sugar on medium speed until creamy. Add the vanilla, then beat in the eggs, one at a time.

2. Gradually beat in flour and salt until well combined. Cover and chill dough for 2 to 3 hours.

3. In a small saucepan over medium heat, combine the remaining ½ cup sugar, cornstarch, cinnamon, dates, raisins, and water. Cook and stir until bubbly and thickened; let cool.

4. To bake the cookies, preheat the oven to 400°F and line cookie sheets with parchment paper.

5. On a lightly floured surface, roll out half the dough until ⅛ inch thick. Cut rounds with a 2-inch cookie cutter and arrange on prepped cookie sheets; reroll the scraps.

6. Spoon a scant 1 teaspoon date filling onto the center of each cookie. Roll out remaining dough and cut rounds as before, but cut another hole in the center of each cookie with a 1-inch cutter.

7. Set "ring" cookies on the rounds with filling and seal the outer edges together with a fork. Bake 10 to 12 minutes, until edges just start to brown.

8. Cool slightly and then remove to wire racks to cool completely. Whisk together the orange extract, zest, powdered sugar, and milk to make a thin glaze.

9. Drizzle over cooled cookies. (These freeze best without the glaze.) Enjoy!

A touch of citrus glaze on these old-fashioned cookies is an excellent update— sweet and so satisfying!

IN A HURRY?

Skip the extra cutting. Just sandwich the filling between two full cookie rounds and seal the edges together. Sweet little pillows!

Orange Fingers

MAKES
4 ½
DOZEN

Ingredients

- 3 ½ cups crushed vanilla wafer cookies
- 2 ¾ cups powdered sugar, sifted
- 1 ½ cups chopped pecans
- 1 (6-ounce) can frozen orange juice concentrate, thawed
- ½ cup butter, melted
- 1 (7-ounce) package shredded coconut

1. In a large bowl, combine the crushed vanilla wafer cookies, sifted powdered sugar, and chopped pecans. Mix well.
2. Stir in orange juice concentrate and melted butter.
3. Shape dough into 2-inch finger shapes. Roll in shredded coconut, place on waxed paper, and refrigerate. Serve when cool and enjoy!

Wonderful White Chocolate Cookies

MAKES
2
DOZEN

Ingredients

- 2 cups white baking chips
- ½ cup chunky peanut butter
- 1 ½ cups miniature marshmallows
- 1 cup unsalted peanuts
- 1 cup Cheerios cereal

1. Melt white baking chips in microwave or a double boiler.
2. Remove from heat and stir in peanut butter. Stir in marshmallows, peanuts, and Cheerios.
3. Drop by teaspoonfuls onto waxed paper. Let cool, cover, and store in refrigerator. Enjoy!

Pistachio-Chocolate Cruncers

Ingredients

- 1 ¼ cups flour
- ½ teaspoon baking soda
- ¼ teaspoon salt
- ½ cup unsalted butter, softened
- ½ cup sugar
- ½ cup brown sugar
- 1 egg
- 1 teaspoon vanilla
- 1 ½ cups dark chocolate chips
- 1 cup shelled, roasted, and salted pistachios, chopped
- Smoked sea salt, for sprinkling

MAKES
4
DOZEN

1. Place the oven rack in the upper third of the oven and preheat to 300°F.

2. Combine the flour, baking soda, and salt in a bowl and set aside. In a big mixing bowl, beat butter, sugar, and brown sugar on medium speed, 3 to 4 minutes.

3. Add egg and vanilla and beat well. Slowly beat in the set-aside flour mixture until combined. Stir in dark chocolate chips and pistachios.

4. Using a 1 ½-inch cookie scoop, drop the dough onto parchment paper–lined cookie sheets, about 2 inches apart. Sprinkle with smoked sea salt and bake 18 to 20 minutes or until golden brown.

5. Cool 5 minutes before removing cookies to a wire rack to finish cooling. (These freeze well.) Serve and enjoy!

Caramel-Nut Clusters

MAKES
2
DOZEN

Ingredients

- ¼ cup butter or margarine
- ½ pound (approximately 28) caramels, wrappers removed
- 2 tablespoons milk
- 3 ½ cups corn flakes cereal
- ½ cup chopped peanuts
- ½ cup shredded coconut

1. In a large saucepan over low heat, combine butter, caramels, and milk. Stir until melted and smooth.

2. Remove from heat and add corn flakes, chopped peanuts, and coconut. Mix well.

3. Drop by tablespoonfuls onto waxed paper. Cookies will harden as they cool. Enjoy!

Chocolate-Butterscotch Drops

MAKES
2
DOZEN

Ingredients

- ½ cup chocolate chips
- 1 butterscotch chips
- 1 cup dry roasted peanuts
- 2 cups Crispix cereal

1. In a large heavy saucepan, melt chocolate chips and butterscotch chips over low heat, stirring constantly.

2. Remove from heat and stir in peanuts and Crispix cereal.

3. Drop by tablespoonfuls onto waxed paper. Cover and store in refrigerator. Enjoy!

Cran-Orange Shortbread

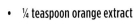

MAKES 2½ DOZEN

Ingredients

- ¾ cup sugar
- 2 ½ cups flour
- 1 cup cold butter, cubed
- ½ cup dried sweetened cranberries
- 1 ¼ teaspoons almond extract, divided
- Zest of 1 orange
- 1 tablespoon orange juice
- ¼ teaspoon orange extract
- ½ cup powdered sugar

1. In a food processor, pulse together the sugar, flour, and butter until very fine crumbs form. Place in a bowl.

2. Place the cranberries into the food processor and pulse to chop; stir the berries into the dough.

3. Stir in 1 teaspoon of almond extract and the zest of 1 orange. Knead dough just until it holds together; shape into a log (2 inches in diameter), wrap tightly in plastic wrap, and chill at least 2 hours.

4. To bake the cookies, preheat the oven to 350°F. Slice dough into ¼-inch-thick rounds and coat in sugar, if you'd like.

5. Arrange on parchment paper–lined cookie sheets and bake 15 minutes or until starting to brown. Cool slightly, then remove to a wire rack until cool.

6. To add a glaze, mix the orange juice, orange extract, remaining ¼ teaspoon almond extract, and the powdered sugar and brush it on. (These freeze well.) Serve and enjoy!

Molasses-Ginger Dips

MAKES 9 DOZEN

Ingredients

- 4 teaspoons cinnamon, divided
- 2 ½ cups sugar, divided
- 1 ½ cups vegetable oil
- 2 eggs
- ½ cup molasses
- 4 cups flour
- 4 teaspoons baking soda
- 1 teaspoon salt
- 1 tablespoon ground ginger
- 1 (12-ounce) package white chocolate chips
- Milk chocolate toffee bits, finely chopped

1. Preheat the oven to 350°F and line cookie sheets with parchment paper. Mix 2 teaspoons of cinnamon and ½ cup of sugar in a small bowl and set aside.

2. In a large mixing bowl, beat together the remaining 2 cups of sugar, oil, eggs, molasses, flour, baking soda, salt, ginger, and remaining 2 teaspoons of cinnamon until well combined.

3. Shape dough into balls by rounded teaspoonful and roll in the set-aside sugar mixture to coat. Place on prepped cookie sheets, 3 inches apart, and bake 8 to 10 minutes. Cool slightly before removing to a wire rack to cool completely.

4. Place the white chips in a small microwaveable bowl and microwave until melted and smooth, stirring every 15 seconds.

5. Dip cookies into the melted chips to partially coat, letting excess drip off. Set dipped cookies aside for a minute or two before dipping the coated edge into the toffee bits; set on waxed paper to dry. (These freeze best before dipping.) Serve and enjoy!

Go beyond ordinary when you ramp up the flavor in these delicious molasses-ginger cookies with white chocolate and toffee bits. Delectable!

Thinnish Mints

**MAKES
2 ½
DOZEN**

Ingredients

- 1 ⅓ cups flour
- ¾ cup unsweetened cocoa powder
- 1 teaspoon baking powder
- ⅛ teaspoon salt
- ¾ cup unsalted butter, softened
- 1 cup sugar

- 1 egg
- 1 teaspoon vanilla
- 1 ¾ teaspoons oil-based peppermint extract, divided
- 1 to 1 ½ (12-ounce) packages dark chocolate candy melts

1. In a bowl, whisk together the flour, cocoa powder, baking powder, and salt; set aside. In a large mixing bowl, beat the butter on medium speed until smooth and creamy. Add the sugar and beat until light and fluffy.

2. Beat in the egg, vanilla, and 1 teaspoon peppermint extract until blended. Slowly beat in the set-aside flour mixture until well combined.

3. Divide dough into two even portions and roll each into a log, 2 inches in diameter. Wrap in plastic wrap and chill for several hours.

4. To bake the cookies, preheat the oven to 350°F and line cookie sheets with parchment paper. Unwrap the dough logs and cut into slices about ⅜ inch thick. Arrange slices on prepped cookie sheets and bake 8 to 10 minutes.

5. Let cool a few minutes before removing to a wire rack to cool completely.

6. To coat the cookies, melt the candy melts according to the package directions and stir in the remaining ¾ teaspoon peppermint extract. Coat each cookie in melted chocolate deliciousness and set on waxed paper, remelting the remaining chocolate as needed for easy coverage.

7. Chill about 15 minutes or until set. Store at room temperature. (Freezing not recommended.) Enjoy!

Bigger and even better than their famous boxed cousins!

3-in-1 Cookies

MAKES 8½ DOZEN

Ingredients

- 2 ½ cups unsalted butter, softened
- 2 cups sugar, plus more for rolling
- 5 ½ cups flour
- 1 ½ teaspoons salt
- 2 ½ teaspoons vanilla
- ½ cup creamy peanut butter
- ½ cup peanuts, finely chopped

- ¾ teaspoon cherry extract, plus more to taste
- ⅓ cup maraschino cherries, drained and diced
- 1 ½ teaspoons melted butter
- ½ cup powdered sugar
- Milk, to taste
- ½ cup mini M&Ms

Prepare one basic dough, divide it into thirds, and customize each portion to create three different types of cookies. It will look like you baked all day—but you didn't!

1. Preheat the oven to 325°F and line cookie sheets with parchment paper.
2. Make the base cookie dough by beating the butter in a large mixing bowl on medium speed until creamy. Gradually beat in the sugar, flour, and salt until light and fluffy. Add vanilla and beat about 5 minutes.
3. Divide the dough evenly among three bowls to prepare three different flavors. (These freeze well.)

Peanut Butter Cookies

MAKES 3 ½ DOZEN

1. To one bowl of dough, stir in creamy peanut butter and chopped peanuts. Shape dough into balls by rounded teaspoonfuls, then roll in sugar.
2. Set on prepped cookie sheets and use a fork to flatten lightly in a crisscross pattern.
3. Bake 15 to 18 minutes and cool on a wire rack. Enjoy!

Cherry Pinwheels

MAKES 2 ½ DOZEN

1. To another bowl of dough, mix in cherry extract. Roll out dough on a lightly floured surface into a ³⁄₁₆-inch-thick rectangle (about 10 x 15 inches) and spread with maraschino cherries.

2. Starting on one long edge, roll dough into a log and freeze until firm. Cut log into ½-inch-thick slices and bake on prepped cookie sheets about 20 minutes.

3. Glaze hot cookies with a mixture of melted butter, powdered sugar, a few drops of cherry extract, and enough milk to make it thin. Let dry on a wire rack. Serve and enjoy!

M&M Favorites

MAKES 2 ½ DOZEN

1. To the last bowl of dough, stir in M&Ms.

2. Use a cookie scoop to drop dough onto prepped cookie sheets and bake 15 to 18 minutes.

3. Cool on a wire rack. Serve and enjoy!

Pecan Tassies

MAKES 2 DOZEN

Ingredients

- ½ cup unsalted butter, softened
- 3 ounces cream cheese, softened
- 1 cup flour
- 1 tablespoon butter, melted
- 1 egg
- ¾ cup light brown sugar
- 1 teaspoon vanilla
- Pinch salt
- ½ cup chopped pecans

1. In a medium mixing bowl, combine the softened butter and cream cheese; beat together on medium speed until smooth and creamy. Beat in the flour until combined. Cover and refrigerate dough for 1 hour.

2. To bake the cookies, preheat the oven to 325°F and coat 24 mini muffin cups with cooking spray.

3. Whisk together the melted butter, egg, brown sugar, vanilla, and salt until smooth. Stir in the pecans and set aside.

4. Roll the dough into 1 inch to 1¼-inch balls and press each one evenly over the bottom and side of a muffin cup for the crust. Spoon a scant tablespoonful of the pecan mixture into each crust.

5. Bake about 18 minutes or until crust is light brown and filling is puffy and set. Cool in pans for 10 minutes before removing to a wire rack to cool completely. (These freeze well.) Serve and enjoy!

Bite-size pecan pies with an oh-so-tender cookie crust—not just for holidays!

Pecan Turtles

MAKES
2½
DOZEN

Ingredients

- 30 miniature chocolate chip cookies or other miniature cookies
- 1 (9-ounce) package caramels, wrappers removed
- 4 teaspoons water
- 2 cups pecan halves
- 1 cup chocolate chips
- ¼ cup chopped pecans, optional

1. Line 2 baking sheets with waxed paper and coat with nonstick cooking spray. Arrange miniature cookies on waxed paper.

2. In a large microwave-safe glass measuring cup, combine caramels with water. Microwave, uncovered, on high for 30 seconds. Stir and microwave for an additional 15 seconds.

3. Top each cookie with ½ teaspoon caramel mixture. Press 4 pecan halves into caramel to resemble turtle feet.

4. Place chocolate chips in a microwave-safe bowl or double boiler. Microwave for 1 minute or heat over stovetop, stirring often, until melted. Stir until smooth.

5. Spoon 1 teaspoon chocolate over each cookie. If desired, sprinkle some chopped pecans over chocolate. Refrigerate at least 45 minutes before serving. Enjoy!

Honey Crunch No-Bakes

MAKES
2
DOZEN

Ingredients

- 3 cups Corn Flakes cereal
- 1 cup powdered sugar
- 1 cup honey
- 1 cup peanut butter
- 1 cup raisins
- 1 ¾ to 2 cups shredded coconut

1. Line a baking sheet with waxed paper.

2. In a large bowl, combine the Corn Flakes, powdered sugar, honey, peanut butter, and raisins. Mix well.

3. Shape mixture into 1-inch balls. Roll in shredded coconut.

4. Place on prepared baking sheet and refrigerate for 1 to 2 hours, until firm. Serve and enjoy!

Raspberry Thumbprints

MAKES 3½ DOZEN

Ingredients

- 1 cup butter, softened
- ⅔ cup sugar
- 2 teaspoons almond extract, divided
- 2 cups flour
- Red raspberry jam, as needed
- 1 cup powdered sugar
- 1 to 2 teaspoons water

1. In a mixing bowl, beat the softened butter just until smooth and creamy. Beat in the sugar and ½ teaspoon of the almond extract until combined.

2. Gradually beat in flour, stirring in any remainder with a spoon. Cover and chill dough for 1 hour.

3. To bake the cookies, preheat the oven to 350°F. Shape dough into 1-inch balls and place on parchment paper–lined cookie sheets. Press your thumb or a wooden spoon handle into the center of each ball to make a deep dent.

4. Fill dents with red raspberry jam and bake about 10 minutes or until edges are light brown. Cool slightly before removing cookies to a wire rack to cool completely.

5. For the icing, mix powdered sugar, 1½ teaspoons of almond extract, and water. Drizzle over cookies and let dry. (These freeze best before icing.) Enjoy!

Tumbleweeds

MAKES
2
DOZEN

Ingredients

- 1 (12-ounce) can salted peanuts
- 1 (7-ounce) can potato sticks
- 3 cups butterscotch chips
- 3 tablespoons peanut butter

1. In a large bowl, combine peanuts and potato sticks and set aside.
2. In a microwave-safe bowl, combine butterscotch chips and peanut butter. Microwave for 1 to 2 minutes, stirring every 30 seconds, until melted.
3. Pour melted mixture over peanut mixture. Stir to coat evenly.
4. Drop by tablespoonfuls onto waxed paper. Refrigerate until set, about 15 minutes. Enjoy!

Chow Mein No-Bakes

MAKES
2
DOZEN

Ingredients

- 2 cups butterscotch chips
- 2 cups chow mein noodles
- 1 cup salted peanuts

1. In a double boiler over simmering water, melt the butterscotch chips, stirring frequently until smooth.
2. Remove from heat and stir in chow mein noodles and peanuts.
3. Drop by teaspoonfuls onto waxed paper and refrigerate until firm. Enjoy!

Butter Pecan Sandies

Ingredients

- 1½ cups chopped pecans
- 1 cup unsalted butter, softened
- ⅓ cup sugar, plus more for rolling
- 2 teaspoons vanilla
- 2 cups flour
- ¼ teaspoon salt
- Powdered sugar, for sprinkling

MAKES 3 DOZEN

1. Preheat the oven to 350°F. Spread the chopped pecans on a rimmed baking sheet and toast the nuts about 6 minutes; let cool.

2. In a mixing bowl, beat the softened butter and sugar until light, about 1 minute. Beat in vanilla, flour, and salt until dough comes together. Knead in the pecans.

3. Shape the dough into 1½-inch balls and roll in more sugar. Arrange on parchment paper-lined cookie sheets and gently flatten with the bottom of a drinking glass.

4. Sprinkle tops with a little more sugar and bake on an upper rack in the oven for 12 to 14 minutes or until bottoms just begin to brown. Cool slightly before removing to a wire rack to finish cooling.

5. Sprinkle with powdered sugar for a nice finishing touch. (These freeze well before sprinkling.) Serve and enjoy!

Sliced Chocolate Swirls

MAKES 4 ½ DOZEN

Ingredients

- 1 cup semi-sweet chocolate chips
- ½ cup sweetened condensed milk
- 1 tablespoon shortening
- ¾ cup butter, softened
- ½ teaspoon salt
- 1 teaspoon almond extract
- ¾ cup light brown sugar
- 2 cups flour
- 2 to 3 teaspoons milk
- ¾ cup chopped almonds or walnuts
- Powdered sugar, optional

1. Preheat the oven to 350°F and line cookie sheets with parchment paper; set aside.

2. In the top of a double boiler, combine the chocolate chips, condensed milk, and shortening; cook over low heat until melted and smooth, stirring often. Let filling cool slightly.

3. Meanwhile, put the butter, salt, almond extract, and brown sugar in a large mixing bowl and beat on medium speed until creamy. Mix in the flour, then stir in the milk as needed until dough holds together.

4. Knead the dough just until smooth and divide into three even portions. On a lightly floured surface, roll out each portion into a 6 x 10–inch rectangle.

5. Spread one-third of the chocolate filling over each rectangle and sprinkle each with ¼ cup almonds. Starting with a long side, roll up the dough and transfer to prepped cookie sheets.

6. Bake 20 to 23 minutes or until light-golden brown. Cool slightly before removing to a wire rack.

7. Cool completely and wrap tightly in plastic wrap.

8. To serve, sprinkle with powdered sugar, if you'd like, and slice diagonally, about ⅜-inch thick. (These freeze well.) Serve and enjoy!

Deliciously different. Crunchy and satisfying. If you love brown sugar cookies, you'll gobble up these pretty treats.

SERVE IT LATER
You can freeze a whole cookie roll after baking—then just defrost and slice for a ready-to-eat treat. Company-worthy, company-ready!

Iced Coconut-Lime Shortbread

MAKES 2½ DOZEN

Ingredients

- ½ cup sweetened flaked coconut
- ½ cup sugar
- 2 tablespoons plus 1 teaspoon lime zest, divided, plus more for sprinkling
- 1 teaspoon clear vanilla
- 2 ½ cups flour
- 1 cup cold butter, sliced
- Water, as needed
- 2 cups powdered sugar
- 1 tablespoon lime juice

1. Preheat the oven to 325°F and line cookie sheets with parchment paper; set aside.

2. In a food processor, combine the coconut, sugar, 2 tablespoons of lime zest, and vanilla; pulse until coconut is finely chopped. Add the flour and pulse to combine. Gradually add the butter pieces and pulse until a smooth dry dough forms.

3. Transfer to a large bowl and knead the dough, adding a teaspoon or two of water as needed to make everything hold together.

4. Divide the dough in half and shape each portion into a ball. On a lightly floured surface, roll out each ball of dough until ¼ inch thick.

5. Cut out rounds with a cookie cutter—big or small, up to you—and place on prepped cookie sheets.

6. Bake 15 to 17 minutes or until bottoms just begin to brown. Cool slightly, then remove to wire racks to cool completely.

7. For the icing, whisk together the powdered sugar, lime juice, 1 teaspoon of zest, and just enough water to make a spreading consistency you like.

8. Spread this zippy icing over the cookies and sprinkle with any remaining zest. Let stand until set. (These freeze best without icing.) Serve and enjoy!

A zippy lime kick
in a light crunchy
cookie— perfect for
summer or anytime!

Apricot Bowties

MAKES
6
DOZEN

Ingredients

- 8 ounces cream cheese, softened
- 1 cup unsalted butter, softened
- ½ teaspoon vanilla
- 1 teaspoon almond extract
- ¾ teaspoon salt
- 2 ½ cups flour

- ¾ cup apricot preserves
- 1 egg, beaten
- ½ cup powdered sugar (optional), plus more for dusting
- 1 tablespoon liquid amaretto coffee creamer (optional)

1. In a large mixing bowl, beat the cream cheese and butter on medium speed for 3 minutes, until light and fluffy.

2. Beat in the vanilla and almond extract. Slowly beat in the salt and the flour until dough forms, stirring in any remainder with a spoon.

3. On a lightly floured surface, knead the dough a few times to form a smooth ball.

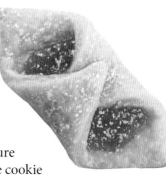

4. Divide dough into thirds, flatten into squares, and wrap each in plastic wrap. Chill at least 4 hours.

5. To bake the cookies, soften dough at room temperature about 15 minutes. Preheat the oven to 400°F and line cookie sheets with parchment paper.

6. Roll out each portion of dough into an 8 x 12–inch rectangle, ⅛ inch thick.

7. With a pizza cutter, trim edges and then cut dough into 2-inch squares; arrange on prepped cookie sheets.

8. Spoon ½ teaspoon of preserves onto the center of each square. Fold one corner to the center, moisten with beaten egg, then fold opposite corner to the center; press and seal with more egg.

9. Bake 10 to 12 minutes, until lightly browned and puffy. Cool slightly before removing to a wire rack to finish cooling.

10. Sprinkle with powdered sugar, or if you prefer, drizzle with a glaze made by mixing ½ cup powdered sugar with 1 tablespoon liquid amaretto coffee creamer. (These freeze best before sprinkling or glazing.) Enjoy!

Don't limit yourself to apricot preserves. These taste great with blueberry, strawberry, cherry... well, you get the idea.

Peanut Crisps

MAKES 6 DOZEN

Ingredients

- 1 cup margarine, softened (not from a tub)
- 1 cup vegetable oil
- 1 cup sugar
- 1 cup brown sugar
- 1 egg
- 1 cup quick-cooking oats
- 1 cup crisp rice cereal

- 1 teaspoon vanilla
- ½ teaspoon salt
- 3 ½ cups flour, divided
- 1 teaspoon baking soda
- 1 teaspoon cream of tartar
- Salted peanuts, halved

1. Preheat the oven to 350°F and line cookie sheets with parchment paper; set aside.

2. In a large mixing bowl, beat the margarine, oil, sugar, brown sugar, and egg on medium speed for 2 or 3 minutes. Add the oats, cereal, vanilla, and salt, beating until well combined.

3. Add 1½ cups flour, baking soda, and cream of tartar and beat well. Slowly beat in as much of the remaining 2 cups flour as possible, stirring in the rest with a spoon if dough gets too stiff.

4. Shape the dough into 1½-inch balls and place on prepped cookie sheets. Flatten slightly and arrange 4 cute little peanut halves on top of each cookie.

5. Bake about 14 minutes or until lightly browned. Let cookies cool a few minutes before removing to a wire rack to cool completely. (These freeze well.) Enjoy!

Tender and crunchy, these old-fashioned peanut cookies will have everyone begging for more!

COOKIES MAKE A GREAT GIFT

These cookies are sturdy enough to stack and pack for successful gift-giving and they freeze well for bake-ahead convenience. Make a bunch to share!

Cathedral Windows

MAKES 2-3 DOZEN

Ingredients

- ½ cup margarine
- 1 (12-ounce) bag chocolate chips
- 1 cup chopped walnuts
- 1 (10.5-ounce) bag colored miniature marshmallows

1. In a double boiler, melt margarine and chocolate chips over low heat, stirring occasionally, until melted and smooth. Let cool slightly.

2. In a large bowl, combine the chopped walnuts, colored marshmallows, and melted chocolate mixture.

3. Prepare five 9-inch sheets of waxed paper.

4. Divide dough into five sections and place one section on each sheet of waxed paper.

5. Roll dough tightly into 2-inch diameter logs and refrigerate overnight. Before serving, unwrap logs and cut into ½-inch slices. Enjoy!

Classic Chocolate Chip

Ingredients

- 2 ¼ cups flour
- 1 teaspoon baking soda
- 2 teaspoons baking powder
- ½ cup softened butter
- ½ cup softened margarine (not from a tub)
- ½ cup sugar
- ½ cup light brown sugar
- 1 (3.4-ounce) package vanilla instant pudding mix
- 1 teaspoon vanilla
- 2 eggs
- 2 cups milk chocolate chips

MAKES 4 ½ DOZEN

1. Preheat the oven to 350°F. Combine the flour, baking soda, and baking powder in a bowl and set aside.

2. In a mixing bowl, beat together the softened butter, softened margarine, sugar, and light brown sugar on medium speed until creamy.

3. On low, beat in the vanilla instant pudding mix and vanilla until combined. Beat in the eggs, then slowly beat in the set-aside flour mixture until just blended.

4. Stir in the milk chocolate chips.

5. Drop the dough by rounded spoonful or cookie scoop onto parchment paper–lined cookie sheets and bake until lightly browned, 9 to 12 minutes.

6. Cool slightly before removing to a wire rack to cool completely. (These freeze well.) Serve and enjoy!

These classic chocolate chip cookies are made extra delicious with my secret ingredient: vanilla pudding!

Glazed Lemon Ricotta Drops

MAKES
4
DOZEN

Ingredients

- 2 ½ cups flour
- 1 teaspoon baking powder
- 1 teaspoon salt
- ½ cup unsalted butter, softened
- 2 cups sugar
- 2 eggs
- 1 (15-ounce) tub whole milk ricotta cheese, room temperature
- Zest and juice of 2 lemons, divided
- 1 ½ cups powdered sugar

1. Preheat the oven to 375°F and line cookie sheets with parchment paper. In a bowl, whisk together the flour, baking powder, and salt; set aside.

2. In a large mixing bowl, beat the butter and sugar on medium speed for 3 minutes, until light and fluffy. Beat in the eggs, one at a time, until blended.

3. Add the ricotta, 1 tablespoon plus 1 teaspoon of lemon zest, and 3 tablespoons of lemon juice; beat well.

4. Gradually beat in as much of the set-aside flour mixture as possible, stirring in the rest with a spoon. Drop the dough by heaping tablespoonful onto prepped cookie sheets and bake 13 to 15 minutes or until slightly golden around edges.

5. Let cool a few minutes before removing to a wire rack to finish cooling.

6. For the glaze, whisk together the powdered sugar, remaining lemon zest, and 2 to 2 ½ tablespoons of the remaining lemon juice until smooth and glaze-like.

7. Spread about ½ teaspoon glaze over each cookie and let dry. (These freeze well before glazing.) Enjoy!

These soft lemon cookies are so mouthwatering and light, they'll be gone before you know it!

Buttery Orange Blossoms

MAKES 4 DOZEN

Ingredients

- ½ cup butter, softened, divided
- 1 cup sugar, divided
- ¾ teaspoon baking soda
- ¾ teaspoon cream of tartar
- ½ teaspoon salt
- 1 egg

- 1 teaspoon orange zest
- ½ teaspoon vanilla
- 1 teaspoon orange extract, divided
- 6 tablespoons olive oil
- ¼ cup white cornmeal

- 2 cups flour
- 1 cup powdered sugar
- 1 tablespoon milk
- Food coloring, as desired

1. In a large mixing bowl, beat 6 tablespoons of butter on high speed, just until creamy. Add ¾ cup sugar, baking soda, cream of tartar, and salt and beat together until light and fluffy.

2. Beat in the egg, zest, vanilla, and ½ teaspoon orange extract until blended. Gradually beat in the oil until smooth.

3. Mix in the cornmeal and as much of the flour as possible, stirring in the rest with a spoon. Cover and chill dough at least 30 minutes.

4. To bake the cookies, preheat the oven to 350°F and line cookie sheets with parchment paper.

5. Pour the remaining ¼ cup sugar into a small bowl. Shape the dough into 1-inch balls and roll in the sugar to coat. Arrange on prepped cookie sheets and press an "X" into each ball of dough with a toothpick.

6. Bake 9 to 12 minutes or until tops are very lightly browned. While warm, press cookies with the toothpick again to deepen the creases. Let cool slightly before removing to a wire rack to finish cooling.

7. For the frosting, whisk together powdered sugar, milk, and the remaining 2 tablespoons butter and ½ teaspoon orange extract until smooth and creamy. Stir in food coloring as desired and pipe a dab of frosting in the center of each cookie. (These freeze well.) Enjoy!

So light and tender, you'll be tempted to eat a whole handful of these sweet blossoms!

Chocolate-Chipotle Oatmeal

MAKES 4 DOZEN

Ingredients

- 2 tablespoons unsweetened cocoa powder
- 1 tablespoon cinnamon
- 1 ¼ cups quick oats, finely ground
- ½ cup cinnamon graham crackers, finely crushed
- ¾ cup flour
- ½ teaspoon baking soda
- ½ teaspoon chipotle chili powder
- ¼ teaspoon salt
- ½ cup butter, softened
- ¼ cup sugar

- 1 cup brown sugar
- 1 egg
- ¾ teaspoon cinnamon extract
- ½ teaspoon vanilla
- ½ cup cinnamon baking chips
- ¼ cup mini semi-sweet chocolate chips
- 1 (1.55-ounce) milk chocolate candy bar, grated
- ½ ounce unsweetened baking chocolate, finely chopped
- Tubinado sugar, to taste

1. Preheat the oven to 350°F and line cookie sheets with parchment paper. Whisk together the cocoa powder, cinnamon, oats, cracker crumbs, flour, baking soda, chili powder, and salt. Set aside.

2. In a large mixing bowl, beat together the butter, sugar, and brown sugar until creamy. Add the egg, cinnamon extract, and vanilla and beat well.

3. Slowly beat in the set-aside flour mixture until combined. Stir in the cinnamon chips and chocolate chips along with grated and chopped chocolates.

4. Shape the dough into 1¼-inch balls and roll in turbinado sugar; arrange on prepped cookie sheets, 2 inches apart.

5. Bake 12 to 15 minutes or until golden brown, then sprinkle with more sugar, if you'd like.

6. Let cool several minutes before removing to a wire rack to cool completely. (These freeze well.) Enjoy!

No-Bake Peanut Butter Bites

Ingredients

- 6 tablespoons melted butter
- ½ teaspoon vanilla
- ⅔ cup plus 2 tablespoons creamy peanut butter, divided

- 2 cups crisp rice cereal
- 1½ cups powdered sugar
- ¼ cup chopped peanuts

- ½ cup 60% cacao bittersweet chocolate chips

1. Line an 8 x 8–inch pan with foil and spritz with cooking spray; set aside.

2. In a bowl, mix the melted butter, vanilla, ⅔ cup of peanut butter, rice cereal, and powdered sugar. Press mixture into prepped pan and press chopped peanuts into the top. Chill at least 1 hour.

3. Lift foil to remove from pan and cut into squares (or cut circles with a small cookie cutter). Set on waxed paper.

4. Combine the chocolate chips and 2 tablespoons of creamy peanut butter in a microwaveable bowl and microwave on 50% power for 45 seconds. Stir and microwave again in 20-second bursts until melted and smooth.

5. Dip the bottom of each bar (not the peanut side) into chocolate, then flip bars chocolate side up and set on waxed paper to dry. Store in refrigerator. (Freezing not recommended.) Serve and enjoy!

Pretzel Scotchies

Ingredients

- 1 cup unsalted butter
- 2 ¼ cups bread flour
- 1 teaspoon salt
- 1 teaspoon baking soda
- 1 cup broken pretzel pieces, divided

- ¼ cup sugar
- 1 ¼ cups dark brown sugar
- 1 egg plus 1 egg yolk
- 2 tablespoons heavy cream or milk
- 1 teaspoon vanilla

- ½ cup butterscotch chips
- ½ cup semi-sweet chocolate chunks

1. In a medium saucepan over low heat, melt the butter; increase the heat to medium and cook until butter turns golden brown, but doesn't burn (watch it closely). Remove from heat and let cool about 20 minutes.

2. Meanwhile, combine the flour, salt, and baking soda in a bowl and finely crush ½ cup of the pretzels; set these aside.

3. Transfer the brown butter to a large mixing bowl and add the sugar and brown sugar; beat on medium speed for 2 to 3 minutes. Beat in the egg and egg yolk until blended.

4. Add the cream and vanilla and beat 2 to 3 minutes more. Gradually beat in the set-aside flour mixture.

5. With a spoon, stir in the butterscotch chips, chocolate chunks, and remaining ½ cup pretzel pieces until evenly combined. Cover and chill dough for 3 hours (or overnight).

6. To bake the cookies, preheat the oven to 350°F and line cookie sheets with parchment paper. Soften the dough at room temperature about 15 minutes.

7. Scoop heaping tablespoons of dough into rough ball shapes and roll lightly in the set-aside crushed pretzels. Place 2 inches apart on prepped cookie sheets and bake 10 to 13 minutes or until golden brown.

8. Let cool 5 minutes before removing to a wire rack to cool completely. (These freeze well.) Serve, crunch, and enjoy!

Butterscotch, chocolate, and pretzels— a sweet-and-salty flavor combo that's irresistible!

COOKIE HACK

A neat trick to make drop cookies prettier is to break the scooped dough in half and reshape it slightly, forcing the glorious chips and pretzels to the top.

Cream Wafers

MAKES 3 DOZEN

Ingredients

- 1 ¼ cups butter, softened, divided
- ⅓ cup heavy cream
- 2 cups flour, plus more as needed
- ¼ cup sugar
- 1 ½ cups powdered sugar, sifted
- 2 teaspoons lemon flavoring
- 2 teaspoons lemon zest
- Milk or lemon juice, optional
- Food coloring, optional

1. In a mixing bowl with a paddle beater, combine 1 cup of the butter, cream, and flour, beating on low speed until well mixed.

2. Divide dough into three even portions, flatten slightly, and wrap each in plastic wrap; refrigerate for 2 hours or until firm.

3. To bake the cookies, preheat the oven to 375°F and line cookie sheets with parchment paper.

4. On a lightly floured surface, roll out one portion of dough until ³⁄₁₆– to ¼ inch thick and cut circles with a 1½-inch round cookie cutter, rerolling scraps; repeat with remaining dough.

5. Pour the sugar into a bowl and coat both sides of cookies with sugar. Arrange on prepped pans and make fork holes in each one.

6. Bake 7 to 10 minutes or until puffy and slightly firm, but not browned. Cool briefly before removing to waxed paper to finish cooling.

7. For the filling, mix the remaining ¼ cup of butter, powdered sugar, lemon flavoring, and zest, adding a little milk or juice if needed to make a thick frosting. Stir in food coloring as desired.

8. Spread about 1 teaspoon frosting between each pair of cookies. (These freeze well.) Enjoy!

Flavor Variations

- **Raspberry-Lemon:** Use raspberry flavoring instead of lemon flavoring and stir in the lemon zest.

- **Toasted Coconut:** Use coconut flavoring instead of lemon flavoring, omit the lemon zest, and stir in 1½ tablespoons toasted coconut.

- **Coconut-Rum:** Use rum flavoring instead of lemon flavoring, omit the lemon zest, and stir in 1½ tablespoons toasted coconut. Mmm . . . tropical paradise!

Sweet frosting between two light and flaky wafer cookies—any color, any flavor, party-perfect!

Brownie Buckeye Cookies

MAKES 2 DOZEN

Ingredients

- 1 cup powdered sugar
- 1 cup creamy peanut butter
- 1 (18.3-ounce) package fudge brownie mix
- ¼ cup butter, melted
- 4 ounces cream cheese, softened
- 1 egg
- 4 ounces chocolate candy coating

1. Preheat the oven to 350°F and line cookie sheets with parchment paper. In a small bowl, mix the powdered sugar and peanut butter until well blended. Shape the mixture into 24 (1-inch) balls. Set aside.

2. In a medium mixing bowl, beat together the brownie mix, butter, cream cheese, and egg on low speed until a dough forms.

3. Drop dough by heaping tablespoonfuls onto prepped cookie sheets to make 24 round cookies. Bake 12 minutes, until tops are dry and slightly cracked.

4. As soon as cookies come out of the oven, lightly press a set-aside peanut butter ball into the center of each one. Let cookies cool 5 minutes before removing to a wire rack to finish cooling.

5. Follow package directions to melt the candy coating in the microwave until smooth. Spoon a little melted chocolate over the peanut butter ball on each cookie.

6. Let stand at room temperature until chocolate is set. (Freezing not recommended.) Enjoy!

SMART BAKING

For chewier drop cookies of any kind, remove them from the oven while centers are still a little soft, then let cookies set up and "finish" baking on the pan a few minutes before removing to a wire rack.

Rich fudge brownie + peanut butter buckeye + chocolate topping = guilty pleasure! Better make plenty of these—they'll disappear fast!

Cheerio No-Bakes

GLUTEN FREE
GLUTEN FREE

MAKES
2
DOZEN

Ingredients

- 2 tablespoons butter
- 1 (10-ounce) package mini marshmallows
- ½ cup crunchy peanut butter (not reduced fat)
- 5 cups Honey Nut Cheerios
- ¾ cup peanut butter M&Ms

1. In a large saucepan over medium heat, melt the butter. Add mini marshmallows and stir until melted.

2. Remove from the heat and stir in the peanut butter. Stir in the Honey Nut Cheerios until completely coated.

3. Carefully fold in the peanut butter M&Ms. Use an ice cream scoop to drop the mixture onto parchment paper and let cool. (Freezing not recommended.) Enjoy!

Chocolate M&M No-Bakes

Ingredients

- ½ cup unsalted butter
- ½ cup milk
- 2 cups sugar
- ¼ cup unsweetened cocoa powder
- ½ cup creamy peanut butter (not reduced fat)
- 1 teaspoon vanilla
- 2 ½ cups quick oats
- 1 cup pretzel M&Ms, coarsely chopped
- ¼ teaspoon sea salt

1. In a medium saucepan over medium-high heat, melt the butter.

2. Stir in the milk, sugar, and cocoa powder and bring to a boil; boil for 1 to 2 minutes, stirring frequently.

3. Remove from heat and stir in the peanut butter and vanilla until smooth. Stir in oats, pretzel M&Ms, and sea salt until combined.

4. Drop the chocolatey mixture by rounded tablespoonfuls onto waxed paper and let cool completely until set. (Freezing not recommended.) Enjoy!

No-Bake Honey Nutters

Ingredients

- 16 graham crackers
- 1 cup crunchy peanut butter
- ⅔ cup honey
- ½ cup powdered milk
- 1 cup shredded coconut

MAKES 4 DOZEN

1. Crush the graham crackers in a food processor or between 2 pieces of wax paper using a rolling pin.

2. In a large mixing bowl, combine peanut butter, honey, and powdered milk. Mix well. Stir in crushed graham crackers.

3. Make small balls with dough and place on waxed paper. Roll balls in shredded coconut. Serve and enjoy!

Classic Chocolate No-Bakes

GLUTEN FREE GLUTEN FREE

MAKES 4 DOZEN

Ingredients

- 2 cups sugar
- 3 tablespoons cocoa powder
- ½ cup margarine
- ½ cup milk
- Pinch of salt
- 3 cups gluten-free oats
- ½ cup peanut butter
- 1 teaspoon vanilla

1. In a large saucepan, bring sugar, cocoa powder, margarine, milk, and salt to a rapid boil for 1 minute.

2. Add the oats, peanut butter, and vanilla.

3. Mix well and remove from heat.

4. Working quickly, drop by teaspoonfuls onto waxed paper and let cool. Enjoy!

Mountain Cookies

Ingredients

- 2 cups sugar
- ½ cup milk
- ½ cup margarine
- 3 tablespoons cocoa powder
- Pinch of salt
- 3 cups gluten-free oats
- ½ cup shredded coconut
- ½ cup crunchy peanut butter
- 1 teaspoon vanilla
- ½ cup dried apricots, chopped

MAKES 2 DOZEN

1. In a large saucepan over medium-high heat, combine sugar, milk, margarine, and cocoa powder.

2. Bring mixture to a boil, stirring frequently, until sugar is completely dissolved.

3. Mix in salt, oats, shredded coconut, peanut butter, vanilla, and apricots.

4. Stir until well combined and drop dough by tablespoonfuls onto waxed paper and let cool. Delicious with a glass of milk!

Sweet Corn Flake No-Bakes

MAKES 3 DOZEN

Ingredients

- 1 cup corn syrup
- 1 cup sugar
- 1 cup creamy peanut butter
- 4 ½ cups Corn Flakes cereal
- 1 cup chocolate chips, optional
- 1 cup butterscotch chips, optional
- Sprinkles, optional

1. In a large saucepan over medium heat, combine the corn syrup and sugar. Bring to a boil for 1 minute and remove from heat.

2. Stir in peanut butter until well blended. Mix in Corn Flakes cereal until evenly coated. Drop by spoonfuls into mini cupcake liners. Cool.

3. For optional drizzle: In a microwave-safe bowl or double boiler, melt chocolate chips and butterscotch chips, stirring often until smooth. Drizzle melted chocolate over cookies. Or, add sprinkles, like I did. Serve and enjoy!

Nut and Fruit Chocolate Drops

MAKES 2 DOZEN

Ingredients

- 1 (12-ounce) package chocolate chips
- ¾ cup cashews, almonds, or macadamia nuts, coarsely chopped
- ¾ cup raisins
- ½ cup dried cranberries or chopped dried apricots

1. In a double boiler over simmering water, melt chocolate chips, stirring until smooth. Remove from heat.

2. Stir in nuts, raisins, and fruit.

3. Drop chocolate mixture by teaspoonfuls onto waxed paper. Let cool until firm, about 2 hours. Enjoy!

Spiked Coffee Snowballs

MAKES 3 DOZEN

Ingredients

- 2 cups prepared sugar cookies, finely crushed
- 1 cup toasted hazelnuts, finely chopped
- 1 ⅓ cups powdered sugar, sifted, divided
- ¼ cup light corn syrup
- 2 tablespoons coffee-flavored liqueur
- 2 tablespoons butter, melted

1. In a medium bowl, combine crushed cookies, toasted hazelnuts, 1 cup powdered sugar, corn syrup, coffee-flavored liqueur, and melted butter. Stir until well mixed.

2. Shape mixture into 1-inch balls.

3. In a shallow bowl, place remaining ⅓ cup powdered sugar. Roll balls in powdered sugar until completely coated and let stand for 2 hours.

4. If desired, roll balls again in powdered sugar right before serving. Chill in refrigerator for 2 days or freeze up to 3 months.

Chocolate Whiskey Truffles

MAKES 2 DOZEN

Ingredients

- 8 ounces chocolate chips
- ½ cup butter
- ⅔ cup gingersnap cookies, finely crushed
- 3 tablespoons whiskey
- ½ cup cocoa powder
- ½ cup powdered sugar

1. In a medium saucepan over low heat, melt chocolate chips and butter, stirring until smooth. Mix in crushed gingersnap cookies and whiskey.

2. Pour mixture into a large bowl. Cover and chill until firm, about 45 minutes.

3. Line baking sheets with foil. Drop truffle mixture by tablespoonfuls onto the foil. Freeze for 15 minutes.

4. Remove from freezer and roll each truffle into smooth rounds.

5. Into a shallow bowl, sift cocoa powder and powdered sugar. Roll each truffle in the cocoa mixture.

6. Cover and refrigerate in an airtight container. Let stand for 15 minutes at room temperature before serving. Enjoy!

Peanut Butter Oatmeal No-Bakes

MAKES 2 DOZEN

Ingredients

- ⅔ cup sugar
- ⅔ cup light corn syrup
- 1 teaspoon vanilla
- 1 ¼ chunky peanut butter
- 3 cups gluten-free oats

1. In a large saucepan over medium heat, combine sugar and corn syrup. Bring to a boil and add vanilla and peanut butter. Stir until well mixed.

2. Gently mix in oats. Drop by tablespoonfuls onto waxed paper.

3. Cookies will harden as they cool. Once cooled, enjoy!

Oatmeal-Cocoa Macaroons

MAKES 2 DOZEN

Ingredients

- ¾ cup butter
- ½ cup milk
- 2 cups sugar
- ½ cup shredded coconut
- 3 cups gluten-free oats
- ½ cup cocoa powder

1. In a saucepan over medium heat, combine butter, milk, and sugar.

2. Stirring constantly, bring mixture to a boil. Continue to boil and stir for 2 minutes.

3. Remove from heat and add coconut, oats, and cocoa powder. Stir until well mixed.

4. Drop by teaspoonfuls onto waxed paper. Chill macaroons in refrigerator. Enjoy!

Chocolate Peanut Butter Bites

MAKES 4½ DOZEN

Ingredients

- 1 cup crunchy peanut butter
- ¼ cup margarine, softened
- 1 cup powdered sugar
- 2 cups Rice Krispies cereal
- 1½ cups chocolate chips
- 2 tablespoons shortening

1. In a large mixing bowl, beat the peanut butter, softened margarine, and powdered sugar at medium speed.

2. Add the Rice Krispies and mix until thoroughly combined.

3. Roll mixture into 1-inch balls. Place one ball in a paper cup, and repeat with the remaining balls, until all dough is gone. Refrigerate.

4. In a small saucepan over low heat, melt chocolate chips and shortening, stirring constantly. Spoon 1 teaspoon of melted chocolate into each paper cup. Refrigerate until firm. Cover and store in refrigerator. Enjoy!

Chocolate Pecan Rum Balls

MAKES 4 DOZEN

Ingredients

- 1 (11-ounce) package chocolate wafer cookies, finely crushed
- 1 ½ cups pecans, finely chopped, plus more as needed
- ½ cup light corn syrup
- ¼ cup light or dark rum
- ½ cup powdered sugar

1. In a large bowl, combine crushed chocolate wafer cookies and chopped pecans.

2. Mix well, and stir in corn syrup and rum. Mix until well combined.

3. Place powdered sugar in a shallow dish. Roll cookie mixture into 1-inch balls and roll balls in powdered sugar, and then in extra chopped pecans. Serve and enjoy!

Snowball No-Bakes

MAKES 2 DOZEN

Ingredients

- 1 cup margarine or butter, softened
- 4 tablespoons water
- 1 teaspoon vanilla
- 6 tablespoons cocoa powder
- 1 ½ cups sugar
- 4 cups gluten-free oats
- Chopped nuts, to taste (I used walnuts)
- Shredded coconut, to taste
- Powdered sugar, as needed

1. In a medium bowl, cream the softened butter, water, and vanilla.

2. Add the cocoa powder, sugar, oats, walnuts, and coconut and mix well.

3. Roll mixture into 1-inch balls. If necessary, add more water to make dough stick together. Roll the balls in powdered sugar. Serve and enjoy!

Salted Caramel No-Bakes

MAKES 2 DOZEN

Ingredients

- 3 tablespoons butter or margarine
- 2 ½ cups miniature marshmallows
- 2 cups pretzel sticks, coarsely broken
- 12 caramel candies, unwrapped

- 1 tablespoon water
- 2 tablespoons peanut butter
- White chocolate drizzle, optional

1. In a heavy saucepan over low heat, melt butter.
2. Add marshmallows and stir until smooth. Remove from heat and mix in broken pretzel sticks until lightly coated.
3. Drop by tablespoonfuls onto waxed paper. In a heavy saucepan over low heat, melt caramels and water, stirring frequently, until smooth.
4. Add peanut butter and mix until well combined. Drizzle mixture over pretzel drops. If you like, drizzle white chocolate on top. Let cool until firm. Crunch and enjoy!

Cookie Bars

Cookie bars have all the flavor with half the effort. And the best part? You can serve these delicious treats right from the pan. Layered, delicious, and easy? Sign me up!

Chocolate Chip

USE A 9" x 9" PAN

Ingredients

- 1 cup butter
- 1 cup brown sugar
- ⅓ cup sugar
- 2 eggs, plus 1 egg yolk, divided
- 1 tablespoon vanilla
- 2⅓ cups flour
- ¼ teaspoon cinnamon
- 1 teaspoon baking soda
- ½ teaspoon salt
- 1 ½ cups semisweet chocolate chips, plus more for sprinkling

1. Preheat the oven to 350°F. Grease or line a 9" x 9" baking pan and set aside.

2. Melt the butter over medium heat and continue heating until golden brown, stirring occasionally so it doesn't burn; transfer to a mixing bowl.

3. Add the brown sugar and sugar and beat on medium speed for 2 minutes until smooth. Mix in the eggs, egg yolk, and vanilla until incorporated.

4. In a separate bowl, whisk together the flour, cinnamon, baking soda, and salt and slowly beat into the butter mixture until just incorporated. Stir in 1½ cups of chocolate chips until just combined.

5. Spread the dough evenly in the pan and sprinkle a handful of chocolate chips over the top. Bake for 20 to 25 minutes, until golden brown.

6. Cool in the pan on a wire rack before cutting into bars. Enjoy!

No-Bake Mocha Bars

USE A 9" x 13" PAN

Ingredients

- ¾ cup butter, softened, divided
- ½ cup sugar
- 1 teaspoon vanilla
- 1 egg
- 2 cups graham cracker crumbs
- ¾ cup shredded coconut
- ½ cup walnuts, finely chopped
- 6 ounces white chocolate
- 2 teaspoons instant coffee grounds
- 2 tablespoons hot strong brewed coffee
- 2 ½ cups powdered sugar
- ¼ cup cocoa powder
- 2 tablespoons milk

1. In a microwave or double boiler over low heat, heat ½ cup of butter, the sugar, vanilla, and egg, stirring often until melted, thickened, and well combined.

2. Add graham cracker crumbs, shredded coconut, and chopped walnuts. Mix well and transfer mixture to a greased 9" x 13" baking dish. Spread evenly and let cool.

3. Meanwhile, to prepare the filling, in a microwave or double boiler over low heat, melt white chocolate, stirring often until smooth. Spread half the melted white chocolate over bottom layer in baking dish.

4. To make the topping, in a medium bowl, dissolve instant coffee grounds in strong brewed coffee. Add powdered sugar, cocoa powder, remaining ¼ cup butter, and milk.

5. Mix well and spread over filling layer in baking dish. Spread the remaining melted white chocolate over filling layer in baking dish.

6. Let cool in refrigerator before cutting into bars. Serve with coffee and enjoy!

Crunchy Fudge Sandwiches

GLUTEN FREE GLUTEN FREE

USE A 9" x 13" PAN

Ingredients

- 2 cups butterscotch chips
- 1 cup creamy peanut butter
- 8 cups Rice Krispies cereal
- 2 cups chocolate chips
- 4 tablespoons butter or margarine
- 1 cup powdered sugar
- 2 tablespoons water

1. Grease a 9" x 13" baking dish and set aside.

2. In a large saucepan over medium heat, melt butterscotch chips and peanut butter, stirring frequently, until smooth. Stir in Rice Krispies cereal.

3. Press half of the mixture into the bottom of prepared pan.

4. In a double boiler, melt chocolate chips and butter, stirring occasionally. Mix in powdered sugar and water, stirring until smooth.

5. Spread chocolate mixture evenly over cereal layer in pan. Top with remaining half of cereal mixture and press down lightly. Cover and refrigerate for about 1 hour before cutting into squares. Enjoy!

Simple Tiger Cookies

USE AN **8″ x 8″** PAN

Ingredients

- 1 (16.5-ounce) roll refrigerated sugar cookie dough
- 1 cup white baking chips
- ½ cup creamy peanut butter
- ½ cup semisweet chocolate chips

1. Preheat the oven to 350°F and grease or line an 8″ x 8″ baking pan.

2. Press the cookie dough evenly into the pan and bake for 15 to 20 minutes, until light golden brown. Cool in the pan on a wire rack.

3. Melt the white baking chips and stir in the peanut butter until well combined then spread evenly over the cooled cookie.

4. Melt the chocolate chips and drizzle over the top of the peanut butter layer. Using a knife, swirl together the chocolate and peanut butter mixtures.

5. Refrigerate until chocolate is set. Set out for a few minutes before cutting into bars. Enjoy!

Yummy Chocolate Oat Bars

USE A 9" x 9" PAN

Ingredients

- 1 cup butter
- ½ cup brown sugar
- 1 teaspoon vanilla
- 3 cups gluten-free oats
- 1 cup chocolate chips
- ½ cup peanut butter

1. Grease a 9" x 9" pan and set aside.

2. In a large saucepan over medium heat, melt butter. Stir in brown sugar and vanilla. Mix in oats.

3. Cook over low heat for an additional 2 to 3 minutes or until ingredients are well blended. Press half of mixture into the bottom of prepared pan.

4. In a small saucepan over low heat, melt chocolate chips and peanut butter, stirring frequently until smooth. Pour chocolate mixture over crust in pan and spread evenly. Crumble remaining half of oat mixture over chocolate layer, pressing in gently.

5. Cover and refrigerate 2 to 3 hours or overnight. Let sit at room temperature before cutting into small bars and serving. Yummy!

M&M Madness Bars

USE A 9" x 13" PAN

Ingredients

- 4 tablespoons margarine
- 1 (10.5-ounce) package miniature marshmallows
- ½ cup peanut butter
- 5 cups Cheerios cereal
- 1 cup M&M candies

1. Grease a 9" x 13" baking dish and set aside.

2. In a large microwave-safe bowl, microwave margarine for 45 seconds or until melted. Add marshmallows and stir to coat. Return to the microwave for an additional 1½ minutes, stirring after 45 seconds.

3. Mix in peanut butter and immediately stir in Cheerios. Add M&Ms and mix well.

4. Transfer mixture to prepared pan and press down with a greased spatula until evenly spread. Allow to cool before cutting into squares and serving. Enjoy!

Lemonade Bars

USE A 13" x 18" PAN

Ingredients

- 2 ⅔ cups plus 4 ½ tablespoons flour, divided
- 1 cup powdered sugar, plus more for sprinkling
- ⅓ cup cornstarch
- ¾ teaspoon salt, plus 1 pinch
- 1 cup plus 2 tablespoons softened butter
- 6 eggs
- 2 cups sugar
- Zest of 2 lemons
- 1 cup lemon juice (4 to 5 lemons)
- ½ cup whole milk

1. Grease or line a 13" x 18" baking pan; set aside.

2. In a big bowl, mix 2 ⅔ cups of the flour, powdered sugar, cornstarch, and salt.

3. Mix in the softened butter until crumbly; press into the prepped pan. Chill for 30 minutes.

4. Preheat the oven to 350°F and bake the chilled cookie for 20 minutes.

5. In a mixing bowl with a whisk attachment, beat the eggs, sugar, and 4 ½ tablespoons of the flour. Add the lemon zest, lemon juice, milk, and a pinch of salt; beat until slightly thickened.

6. Pour over warm crust, reduce oven temperature to 325°F, and bake for 18 to 20 minutes, until slightly firm. Cool in the pan on a wire rack.

7. Sprinkle powdered sugar over the top before cutting into bars. Serve and enjoy!

Choco-PB Bars

USE A 10" x 15" PAN

Ingredients

- 10 graham crackers
- ⅔ cup butter, melted
- 2 cups powdered sugar
- 1 cup crunchy peanut butter
- 2 cups chocolate chips

1. Line the bottom of a 10" x 15" jellyroll pan with graham crackers.

2. In a medium bowl, cream together melted butter, powdered sugar, and peanut butter until smooth. Spread mixture over graham crackers and chill until firm, about 15 minutes.

3. In microwave or a double boiler, melt chocolate chips, stirring frequently. Spread melted chocolate over layer of chilled peanut butter mixture.

4. Refrigerate until firm and cut into squares. Place bars between layers of waxed paper in an airtight container in refrigerator. Enjoy!

Funky Frito Bars

GLUTEN FREE GLUTEN FREE

USE A 10" x 15" PAN

Ingredients

- 1 (14.5-ounce) bag of Fritos corn chips, slightly crushed
- 1 cup sugar
- 1 cup light corn syrup
- 1 cup creamy peanut butter
- 11 (1.55-ounce) milk chocolate bars or 1½ (11.5-ounce) packages milk chocolate chips

1. In a greased 10" x 15" jellyroll pan, place Fritos.

2. In a medium saucepan over medium heat, bring sugar and corn syrup to a boil. Remove from heat and stir in peanut butter until smooth.

3. Pour mixture over corn chips and spread evenly. Place chocolate bars in a single layer over hot mixture and let melt for a few minutes before smoothing chocolate out to form a thin layer.

4. Let cool before breaking into pieces and serving.

Sea-Salted Chocolate Cookies

USE AN 8" x 8" PAN

Ingredients

- 1 (10-ounce) package caramels, unwrapped
- ¼ cup whipping cream
- ¾ cup butter, softened
- 1 ¼ cups brown sugar
- 1 teaspoon vanilla
- 1 egg, lightly beaten
- 1 ½ cups flour
- ½ teaspoon baking powder
- ¼ teaspoon baking soda
- ¾ teaspoon coarse sea salt, divided
- 1 cup dark chocolate chips

1. Preheat the oven to 350°F. Grease or line an 8" x 8" baking pan and set aside.

2. In a double boiler over simmering water, heat the caramels and whipping cream together, stirring often, until melted and smooth; set aside to cool.

3. In a mixing bowl, cream together the butter and brown sugar then mix in the vanilla and egg.

4. In a separate bowl, whisk together the flour, baking powder, baking soda, and ¼ teaspoon of the sea salt and add it slowly to the creamed mixture. Stir in the chocolate chips until just combined.

5. Press half of the dough into the prepped pan, pour the caramel mixture evenly over the dough, and sprinkle with the remaining ½ teaspoon sea salt.

6. Put blobs of the remaining dough over the top and spread gently. Bake for 15 to 20 minutes, until set.

7. Cool in the pan on a wire rack before cutting into bars. Enjoy with a glass of milk!

No double boiler? Put about 1 inch of water into a saucepan and set a heatproof bowl on top, making sure the bowl doesn't touch the water. Heat the caramels and whipping cream as directed.

Sugar Cookie Squares

USE A 9" x 13" PAN

Ingredients

- ½ cup plus 5 tablespoons butter, softened, divided
- 1 cup sugar
- 1 egg
- 2 tablespoons sour cream
- 1 teaspoon plus 1 tablespoon vanilla, divided
- 2 ½ cups flour
- ½ teaspoon baking powder
- ½ teaspoon salt
- 3 to 4 tablespoons whipping cream
- 4 cups powdered sugar
- Pinch of salt
- Food coloring and nonpareils, optional

1. Preheat the oven to 375°F. Grease or line a 9" x 13" baking pan and set aside.

2. To make the cookie, in a big mixing bowl, beat ½ cup of butter and sugar together until light and fluffy. Add the egg, sour cream, and 1 teaspoon of the vanilla and mix well.

3. In a separate bowl, whisk together the flour, baking powder, and salt and add it slowly to the creamed mixture, mixing until just combined.

4. Press the dough evenly into the prepped pan and bake for 15 to 17 minutes or until the edges are just golden brown. Cool in the pan on a wire rack.

5. For the frosting, beat together the 5 tablespoons of butter, 1 tablespoon vanilla, whipping cream, powdered sugar, and salt until nice and creamy. Stir in food coloring if using.

6. Spread over the cooled cookie base and top with nonpareils if using. Cut into bars.

Fun Variations

- **Halloween:** Tint the frosting bright orange and toss on decorating sprinkles and googly candy eyes.

- **Circus Animals:** Carefully stir some frosted animal cookies and ¼ cup decorating sprinkles (the long skinny kind) into dough before baking.

- **Confetti:** Stir ½ cup decorating sprinkles (the long, skinny kind) into the dough before baking; add more on the frosting.

Monster Cookie Bars

USE A
13" x 18"
PAN

GLUTEN FREE
GLUTEN FREE

Ingredients

- 4 eggs
- 1 ½ cups sugar
- 1 cup brown sugar
- ¾ teaspoon salt
- 2 ½ teaspoons baking soda
- 1 tablespoon vanilla
- 2 cups crunchy peanut butter
- 5 tablespoons butter, softened
- 1 (16- to 18-ounce) container gluten-free oats
- 1 cup peanut butter chips
- 1 ¼ cups M&Ms, divided

1. Preheat the oven to 350°F. Grease or line a 13" x 18" baking pan and set aside

2. In a big mixing bowl, beat together the eggs, sugar, brown sugar, salt, and baking soda until well combined. Add the vanilla, peanut butter, and butter, beating until smooth.

3. Stir in the oats, peanut butter chips, and 1 cup of the M&Ms until combined. Spread evenly into the prepped pan and sprinkle the remaining ¼ cup M&Ms on top.

4. Bake for 15 to 20 minutes, until golden brown and the center is set. Cool in the pan on a wire rack before cutting into bars. Enjoy!

Coffee Shortbread

Ingredients

USE A 9" x 13" PAN

- 1 ¼ cups butter, softened, divided
- ½ cup plus 1 tablespoon sugar
- 1 teaspoon vanilla
- ¼ teaspoon salt, plus 1 pinch, divided
- 2 ¼ cups plus 2 tablespoons flour
- 1 tablespoon finely ground coffee
- ⅓ cup brown sugar
- 1 tablespoon strong brewed coffee or espresso
- 1 tablespoon light corn syrup
- 40 chocolate-covered coffee beans, optional

1. Preheat the oven to 300°F and line a 9" x 13" baking pan with parchment paper, letting it hang over the sides of the pan; set aside.

2. In a mixing bowl, beat 1 cup of the butter with the sugar until creamy. Beat in the vanilla and ¼ teaspoon salt until well blended.

3. In a separate bowl, whisk together the flour and ground coffee; add it to the butter mixture, a little at a time, mixing until just combined.

4. Press the dough evenly into the prepped pan. Bake for 45 to 50 minutes or until very lightly browned. Set the pan on a wire rack for 10 minutes then use a plastic knife to cut into bars and let cool.

5. For the butterscotch glaze: In a small heavy saucepan over medium heat, mix the brown sugar, brewed coffee, corn syrup, a pinch of salt, and the remaining ¼ cup butter.

6. Bring to a boil and boil for 3 to 4 minutes, until slightly thickened, stirring constantly; remove from the heat and pour over the shortbread, spreading evenly.

7. With a knife, score along the cut lines. Press a coffee bean into the center of each bar. Cool slightly before lifting the parchment to remove from the pan. Cut along the score marks. Serve and enjoy!

Chocolate Chip Crispies

USE A
9" x 13"
PAN

Ingredients

- 1 cup corn syrup
- 1 cup sugar
- 1 ½ cups peanut butter
- 8 cups Rice Krispies cereal
- 1 cup chocolate chips

1. Grease a 9" x 13" pan and set aside.

2. In a large microwave-safe bowl, combine corn syrup, sugar, and peanut butter. Microwave on high until mixture begins to boil, about 2 to 3 minutes.

3. Remove from microwave and stir in Rice Krispies and chocolate chips until well coated. Pour mixture into prepared pan.

4. Press down with a greased spatula until smoothed. Let cool before cutting into squares and serving!

Peanut Chewies

USE A
10" x 15"
PAN

Ingredients

- 1 cup corn syrup
- ¾ cup peanut butter
- 1 ½ cups chocolate chips
- 1 teaspoon vanilla
- 2 ½ cups gluten-free oats
- 1 ¾ cups unsalted peanuts

1. In a medium saucepan over medium heat, combine corn syrup, peanut butter, and chocolate chips. Bring to a boil, stirring constantly.

2. Continue to boil for 5 minutes. Remove from heat and stir in vanilla, oats, and peanuts.

3. Turn onto a greased 10" x 15" jellyroll pan. Let mixture slightly cool before pressing down into pan.

4. Refrigerate overnight. Let stand for 20 minutes before cutting into squares and serving.

Fudgy Potato Chip Bars

USE A 9" x 13" PAN

Ingredients

- 1 ½ cups plus 1 tablespoon softened butter, divided
- 1 ½ cups sugar
- 2 eggs
- 1 tablespoon vanilla
- 3 cups flour
- 1 ½ teaspoons baking powder
- ½ teaspoon salt
- 2 ½ cups potato chips, crushed, divided
- 1 (14-ounce) can sweetened condensed milk
- 2 cups semisweet chocolate chips

1. Preheat the oven to 350°F. Grease or line a 9" x 13" baking pan; set aside.

2. In a mixing bowl, beat together 1 ½ cups of the softened butter and the sugar until light and fluffy. Add the eggs and vanilla and beat until combined.

3. Stir together the flour, baking powder, and salt and add to the creamed mixture, a little at a time, beating until just combined.

4. Stir in 1 ½ cups of the crushed potato chips and press into the prepped pan.

5. Bake for 30 to 35 minutes, until golden brown. Cool in the pan on a wire rack for about an hour.

6. For the fudge frosting: In a microwave-safe bowl, combine the sweetened condensed milk, semi-sweet chocolate chips, and the remaining butter. Microwave on high for 1 ½ minutes until melted and smooth, stirring every 30 seconds; spread evenly over cookie and sprinkle with 1 cup of crushed potato chips (if serving the same day).

7. Chill before cutting into bars. Serve, crunch, and enjoy.

No-Bake Butterscotch Bars

USE A
9" x 13"
PAN

Ingredients

- 3 tablespoons butter or margarine
- 1 (10.5-ounce) package marshmallows
- 3 tablespoons instant butterscotch pudding mix
- 6 cups Rice Krispies cereal

1. In a large saucepan over low heat, melt butter. Add marshmallows and stir until completely melted.

2. Remove from heat. Stir in butterscotch pudding mix. Add Rice Krispies cereal, stirring until completely coated.

3. Using a greased spatula, press mixture evenly into a greased 9" x 13" pan. Let cool before cutting into 2-inch squares. Serve immediately.

Cherry Mash

USE A
9" x 9"
PAN

Ingredients

- 2 tablespoons butter
- 1 cup sugar
- ¼ teaspoon salt
- ⅓ cup half-and-half
- 1 cup miniature marshmallows
- 1 cup cherry baking chips
- 1 cup chocolate chips
- ½ cup peanut butter
- 1 cup roasted Spanish peanuts

1. Line a 9" x 9" square pan with waxed paper and set aside.

2. In a medium saucepan, combine butter, sugar, salt, and half-and-half. Heat until boiling, stirring occasionally.

3. Boil for 5 minutes, being sure to stir often enough to keep from scorching. Remove from heat and stir in marshmallows and cherry baking chips. Press mixture into prepared pan.

4. In microwave or double boiler, melt chocolate chips and peanut butter, stirring frequently until smooth. Mix in roasted Spanish peanuts. Spread chocolate mixture over mixture in pan.

5. Refrigerate 2 hours before cutting into squares and serving. Enjoy!

Mint Chocolate Yums

USE AN
8" x 8"
PAN

Ingredients

- 1 ½ cups semisweet chocolate chips
- ½ cup milk chocolate chips
- 2 teaspoons shortening
- ¾ cup sweetened condensed milk, divided
- 1 cup white baking chips
- 2 ½ teaspoons peppermint extract
- Green food coloring

1. Line an 8" x 8" pan with foil; spray with nonstick cooking spray and set aside.

2. In a saucepan over low heat, melt together both kinds of chocolate chips, shortening, and ½ cup of the sweetened condensed milk, stirring until smooth; spread half evenly into prepped pan and chill for 10 minutes.

3. In a small saucepan over low heat, melt together the white baking chips and the remaining ¼ cup sweetened condensed milk, stirring until smooth.

4. Remove from heat and stir in peppermint extract and food coloring to desired shade. Spread evenly over chocolate layer in the pan. Spread the remaining chocolate over the top. Refrigerate until set, about 2 hours.

5. Remove from pan by lifting foil. Cut into bars. Serve and enjoy!

Toffee Cheesecake Bars

USE A 9" x 13" PAN

Ingredients

- ½ cup butter
- 1 (17.5-ounce) package sugar cookie mix
- 1 (3-ounce) package French vanilla instant pudding mix
- 2 tablespoon brown sugar
- 2 ½ teaspoons vanilla, divided

- 2 eggs, divided
- 2 (8-ounce) packages cream cheese, softened
- ½ cup sour cream
- ½ cup sugar
- 3 egg yolks
- ⅔ cup toffee bits, crushed

1. Preheat the oven to 350°F. Grease or line a 9" x 13" baking pan and set aside.

2. In a big microwave-safe bowl, melt the butter in the microwave; let it cool for a few minutes. Add the cookie mix, pudding mix, brown sugar, vanilla, and one egg, stirring until well combined and a soft dough forms.

3. Press evenly into the prepped pan, creating a ½-inch rim all the way around to hold the filling.

4. For the filling: In a mixing bowl, beat together the cream cheese, sour cream, and sugar on medium speed until smooth.

5. Add the remaining egg and egg yolks one at a time, beating well after each addition; beat in the remaining vanilla until smooth and spread evenly over the cookie base. Bake for 30 to 35 minutes, until set in the center.

6. Immediately sprinkle the toffee bits over the top. Cool for 30 minutes then refrigerate for several hours until chilled.

7. Cut into bars, serve, and enjoy!

3 Oatmeal Cookie Bars

Oatmeal Raisin

Ingredients

- ½ cup butter
- 1 cup flour
- ½ cup sugar
- ½ cup brown sugar

- ½ teaspoon baking soda
- ½ teaspoon salt
- ½ teaspoon cinnamon
- ¼ teaspoon ground nutmeg

- 1 teaspoon vanilla
- 1 egg
- 2 cups quick-cooking oats
- 1½ cups raisins

1. Preheat the oven to 350°F and grease or line an 8" x 8" baking pan; set aside.

2. Melt the butter and set aside to cool slightly. In a big bowl, whisk together the flour, sugar, brown sugar, baking soda, salt, cinnamon, and nutmeg.

3. Make a well in the center of the dry ingredients and add the vanilla, egg, and the set-aside melted butter; stir until smooth.

4. Stir in the oats and raisins until well combined. Spread mixture evenly into prepped pan and bake for 22 to 26 minutes, until the edges are golden brown.

5. Cool in the pan on a wire rack before cutting into bars. Enjoy!

Jammies

Ingredients

- ½ cup brown sugar
- 1 cup flour
- ¼ teaspoon baking soda

- ⅛ teaspoon salt
- 1 cup old-fashioned oats
- ½ cup softened butter

- ¾ cup raspberry preserves

1. Preheat the oven to 350°F and grease or line an 8" x 8" baking pan; set aside.

2. In a bowl, stir together the brown sugar, flour, baking soda, salt, and oats. Add softened butter and use your hands or a pastry blender to crumble it into the flour mixture.

3. Press 2 cups of the mixture into the prepped pan.

4. Stir the raspberry preserves (or your favorite flavor) and spread over the top, to within ¼ inch of the edges; sprinkle the remaining crumbly mixture over the preserves.

5. Bake for 35 to 40 minutes, until lightly browned. Cool in the pan on a wire rack before cutting into bars. Enjoy!

Oatmeal Raisin

Jammies

White Chocolate Cranberry

White Chocolate Cranberry

Ingredients

USE A
9" x 13"
PAN

- 2 ½ cups old-fashioned oats
- 2 cups flour
- 1 ½ cups brown sugar
- 1 teaspoon baking soda

- 1 teaspoon salt
- 1 tablespoon vanilla
- 1 egg
- 2 egg whites

- 1 ¼ cups melted butter
- 1 cup white baking chips
- 1 cup dried cranberries

1. Preheat the oven to 350°F and grease or line a 9" x 13" baking pan; set aside.

2. In a mixing bowl, mix the oats, flour, brown sugar, baking soda, salt, vanilla, egg, egg whites, and melted butter until just combined.

3. Stir in white baking chips and cranberries. Spread evenly into prepped pan and bake for 25 to 30 minutes or until a toothpick inserted into the center comes out with a few moist crumbs.

4. Cool in the pan on a wire rack before cutting into bars. Enjoy!

Blueberry Ice Cream Sammies

USE A 9" x 13" PAN

Ingredients

- 1 cup butter, softened
- ½ cup powdered sugar
- 1 teaspoon vanilla
- 2 cups flour
- ½ cup cornstarch
- ½ teaspoon salt
- 1 (4-ounce) package dried blueberries (about ¾ cup)
- Block-style ice cream (I used cheesecake flavored)

1. Preheat the oven to 350°F and line a 9" x 13" baking pan with parchment paper; set aside.

2. In a mixing bowl, cream together the butter, powdered sugar, and vanilla.

3. In a separate bowl, whisk together the flour, cornstarch, and salt and add slowly to the butter mixture, beating until just combined. Stir in the dried blueberries and spread evenly into the prepped pan.

4. Bake for 25 to 30 minutes, until light golden brown. Cool for 20 minutes.

5. While the cookie is still warm, carefully lift the parchment paper to remove from the pan. Set on a cutting board and cut into 18 pieces (3 rows by 6 rows); set aside to cool.

6. Cut the ice cream into ½-inch-thick slices then cut the slices into nine blocks the same size as the cookies.

7. Carefully set one ice cream block onto half the cooled cookies then top with the remaining cookies. Freeze until firm.

8. Wrap individually in plastic wrap until ready to eat. Enjoy!

Homemade Baby Ruths

USE A 9" x 13" PAN

Ingredients

- 1 cup peanut butter
- 1 cup white corn syrup
- ½ cup brown sugar
- ½ cup sugar
- 6 cups Corn Flakes cereal
- 1 cup chocolate chips
- ⅔ cup peanuts

1. In a large saucepan over medium heat, combine peanut butter, corn syrup, brown sugar, and sugar.

2. Cook, stirring occasionally, until smooth. Remove from heat and quickly mix in Corn Flakes, chocolate chips, and peanuts until evenly coated.

3. Press entire mixture gently into a greased 9" x 13" baking dish. Allow to cool completely before cutting into bars and enjoying!

No-Bake Butterfingers

USE A 9" x 13" PAN

Ingredients

- ⅔ cup sugar
- ⅔ cup light corn syrup
- 1 (16-ounce) jar crunchy peanut butter
- 3 cups Corn Flakes cereal
- 2 cups milk chocolate chips

1. In a heavy saucepan over medium heat, combine sugar and syrup until boiling.

2. Add the peanut butter. Mix until well blended.

3. Remove from heat and stir in Corn Flakes, making sure to coat well. Press mixture into a greased 9" x 13" pan.

4. In a small saucepan over low heat, melt the chocolate chips. Spread melted chocolate over ingredients in pan.

5. Let chill for 20 to 25 minutes before cutting into bars. Serve and enjoy!

Cappuccino Cookie Bars

USE A 9" x 13" PAN

Ingredients

- 7 tablespoons instant cappuccino mix (I used mocha flavored)
- 2 ½ tablespoons hot water
- 1 cup butter, softened
- ¾ cup sugar
- 1 egg yolk (lightly beaten)
- 2 ½ cups flour
- Pinch of salt
- 2 (4-ounce) packages white baking chocolate

1. Preheat the oven to 375°F and grease or line a 9" x 13" baking pan; set aside.

2. In a small bowl, stir together the cappuccino mix and water to make a paste; set aside. In a mixing bowl, combine the butter and sugar; beat until smooth.

3. Beat in the egg yolk and the set-aside cappuccino mixture. Stir together the flour and salt and add slowly to the creamed mixture, beating until combined; press dough evenly into prepped pan and bake for 20 minutes, until set.

4. Cool in the pan on a wire rack.

5. Melt the white chocolate; set aside ¼ cup and spread the remainder over the cooled cookie.

6. When just beginning to set, score where you want the bars cut. When hardened, cut along score marks; drizzle with the set-aside chocolate, re-melting as needed. Serve and enjoy!

Cherry Coconut Concoction

USE A 9" x 9" PAN

Ingredients

- ¼ cup butter or margarine
- 1 (10.5-ounce) package miniature marshmallows
- 5 cups Rice Krispies cereal
- 1 cup shredded coconut
- ½ cup peanuts, coarsely chopped, optional
- ½ cup maraschino cherries, chopped

1. In a large saucepan over low heat, melt butter. Add marshmallows and stir until completely melted. Remove from heat.

2. Add Rice Krispies cereal, coconut, peanuts (if using), and chopped cherries, stirring until completely coated.

3. Using a greased spatula, press mixture evenly into a greased 9" x 9" pan. Let cool in refrigerator for 30 minutes before cutting into bars. Enjoy!

Caramel Cashew Crunchies

USE A 9" x 13" PAN

Ingredients

- 1 (14-ounce) bag caramels, wrappers removed
- 2 tablespoons butter or margarine
- 6 cups Cocoa Krispies cereal
- 1 cup cashews
- 1 cup white baking chips, divided

1. In a large microwave-safe bowl, combine caramels, butter, and 2 tablespoons water. Microwave on high for 3 minutes, stirring after each minute, until melted and smooth.

2. Add Cocoa Krispies cereal and cashews. Stir until well coated.

3. Add ½ cup white baking chips, stirring until well combined.

4. Spread mixture into a greased 9" x 13" pan. Let stand for 2 minutes.

5. Sprinkle remaining ½ cup white baking chips over mixture and press evenly into pan. Let cool before cutting into 2-inch squares. Cut, serve, and enjoy!

7-Layer S'mores

Ingredients

- 1 ½ cups pretzel crumbs
- ½ cup graham cracker crumbs
- ¼ cup brown sugar
- ½ cup melted butter
- 1 (7-ounce) jar marshmallow crème

- 24 Oreo cookies
- 1 cup crunchy peanut butter
- 1 ½ cups mini M&Ms
- ¾ cup sweetened condensed milk
- 2 cups mini marshmallows

USE A
9" x 13"
PAN

1. Preheat the oven to 350°F and grease or line a 9" x 13" baking pan; set aside.

2. Stir together the pretzel crumbs, graham cracker crumbs, brown sugar, and melted butter; press mixture into prepped pan.

3. Drop the marshmallow crème by spoonfuls over the base. Arrange the Oreos evenly over the crème layer and put the crunchy peanut butter in blobs over the cookies; sprinkle with the mini M&Ms. Drizzle the sweetened condensed milk over everything and bake for 25 minutes.

4. Cool for 10 minutes then scatter the mini marshmallows over the top and put under a hot broiler for 20 to 30 seconds to lightly toast the marshmallows.

5. Cool completely then refrigerate for a couple of hours before cutting into bars.

Tropical Twist

USE AN 8" x 8" PAN

Ingredients

- 24 vanilla sandwich cookies
- ¼ cup butter, melted
- 1 (4-ounce) package macadamia nuts, chopped
- 1 cup white baking chips, plus more for sprinkling
- 1 cup unsweetened coconut flakes, plus more for sprinkling
- 1 (6-ounce) package dried pineapple, chopped
- 1 (14-ounce) can sweetened condensed milk

1. Preheat the oven to 325°F. Grease or line an 8" x 8" baking pan and set aside.

2. Put the cookies and butter into a food processor and blend until finely crushed. Dump the crumbs into the prepped pan and press evenly. Bake for 10 minutes.

3. Remove the pan from the oven and increase oven temperature to 350°F.

4. Sprinkle the nuts over the cookie, followed by 1 cup baking chips, 1 cup coconut, and the dried pineapple. Drizzle the sweetened condensed milk evenly over everything and sprinkle with more baking chips and coconut.

5. Bake for 25 to 30 minutes or until the edges are golden brown. Cool completely before cutting into bars. Enjoy!

Unsweetened coconut is drier and chewier than the sweetened kind, and the larger flakes give these bars a fun texture. You could use sweetened if you prefer.

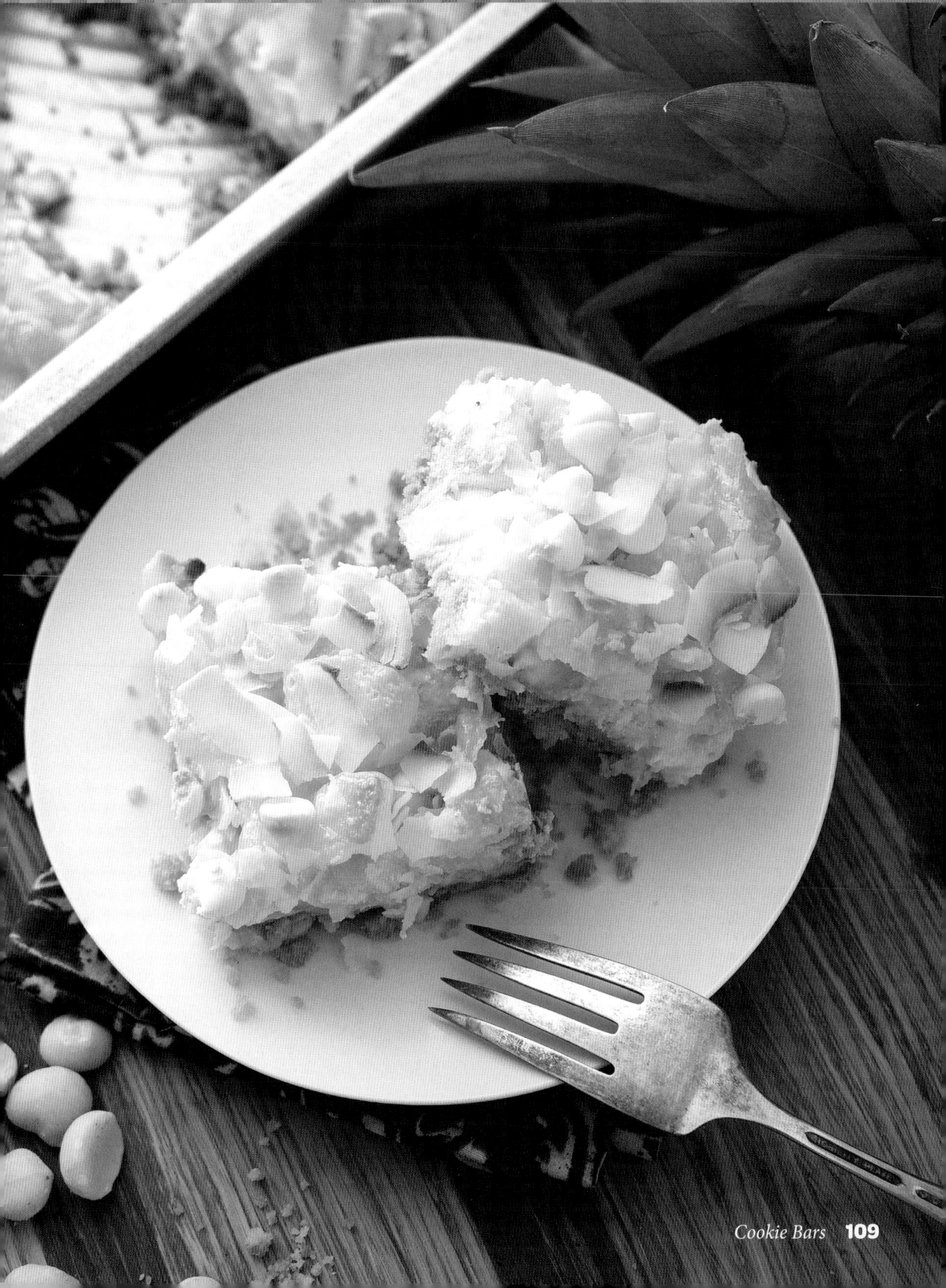

Honey Bunches of PB Oats

Ingredients

- 1 (16-ounce) package Honey Bunches of Oats cereal
- 1 cup sugar
- 1 cup light corn syrup
- 1 cup peanut butter

1. In a large bowl, place the Honey Bunches of Oats cereal and set aside.

2. In a medium microwave-safe bowl, combine the sugar, corn syrup, and peanut butter. Microwave on high for 4 to 5 minutes, until mixture begins to boil.

3. Pour mixture over cereal and stir until well coated. Press mixture into a greased 9" x 13" pan.

4. Let cool before cutting into bars and serving.

Crispy Kiss Squares

Ingredients

- 6 cups Cocoa Puffs cereal
- ¼ cup butter or margarine
- 40 large marshmallows
- 1 (11.5-ounce) package chocolate chips
- 24 striped Hershey's Kisses candies, unwrapped

1. In a large bowl, place Cocoa Puffs cereal and set aside.

2. In a microwave-safe bowl, combine butter and marshmallows. Microwave on high for 3 minutes. Stir and continue heating, as needed, until smooth, stirring after every minute.

3. Add chocolate chips and mix until chocolate chips are completely melted. Pour melted mixture over cereal in bowl.

4. Spread mixture evenly into a 9" x 13" baking dish. Place the Hershey's Kisses in rows over the top.

5. Let cool completely before cutting into squares, serving, and enjoying.

Caramel Apple Cookie Bars

USE A 10" x 15" PAN

Ingredients

- 1 ⅔ cups flour, plus 1 tablespoon, divided
- 1 ½ cups old-fashioned oats
- ⅔ cup brown sugar, plus 2 tablespoons, divided
- ¾ cups butter, plus 1 tablespoon, sliced
- 1 tablespoon sugar
- 2 (8-ounce) packages cream cheese, softened
- 1 cup caramel dip
- 1 egg
- 1 teaspoon vanilla
- 2 Granny Smith apples, peeled and chopped

1. Grease or line a 10" x 15" baking pan; set aside.

2. Combine 1 ⅔ cups of flour, the oats, and ⅔ cup of brown sugar. Cut in the butter until crumbly.

3. Set aside ¾ cup of the mixture and stir the sugar into it; press the remainder into the prepped pan.

4. Bake the cookie for 10 to 12 minutes, until light brown; set aside but don't shut off the oven.

5. In a mixing bowl, beat the cream cheese until creamy. Mix in the caramel dip. Beat in 2 tablespoons of brown sugar, 1 tablespoon of flour, the egg, and the vanilla; pour mixture over warm crust.

6. Arrange the apples over the cream cheese mixture, pressing lightly. Bake for 15 to 20 minutes, until set.

7. Sprinkle the set-aside crumbly mixture over the apples and broil until just browned.

8. Cool completely then chill until firm before cutting into bars. Drizzle with more caramel dip if you'd like. Enjoy!

3 Peanut Butter Cookie Bars

Basic PB

Ingredients

- ½ cup sugar
- ½ cup brown sugar
- ½ teaspoon baking soda
- ¼ teaspoon salt
- 1 cup creamy peanut butter
- 1 egg
- 1 teaspoon vanilla

USE AN 8" x 8" PAN

1. Preheat the oven to 350°F and grease or line an 8" x 8" baking pan; set aside.

2. In a mixing bowl, stir together the sugar, brown sugar, baking soda, and salt.

3. Beat in the creamy peanut butter, egg, and vanilla until combined. Spread the dough evenly into the prepped pan and make a crisscross pattern with a fork if you'd like.

4. Bake for 15 to 18 minutes or until the edges are light golden brown; they will appear jiggly in the middle but will set as they cool.

5. Cool in the pan on a wire rack before cutting into bars. Enjoy!

Oatmeal PB

Ingredients

- ½ cup softened butter
- ¾ cup creamy peanut butter
- ½ cup brown sugar
- ½ cup sugar
- 1 egg
- 1 teaspoon vanilla
- 1 cup flour
- ½ cup oats
- 1 teaspoon baking soda
- ¼ teaspoon salt
- ½ cup peanut butter chips, plus a handful for sprinkling

USE A 9" x 9" PAN

1. Preheat the oven to 350°F and grease or line a 9" x 9" baking pan; set aside.

2. In a mixing bowl, cream together the softened butter, peanut butter, brown sugar, and sugar until light and fluffy. Beat in the egg and vanilla.

3. In a separate bowl, whisk together the flour, oats, baking soda, and salt. Add the flour mixture, a little at a time, to the butter mixture and beat until just incorporated.

4. Stir in the peanut butter chips. Spread the mixture into the prepped pan and sprinkle a handful of peanut butter chips over the top.

5. Bake for 30 to 35 minutes, until the center is just set. Cool in the pan on a wire rack before cutting into bars. Enjoy!

Basic PB

Loaded PB

Oatmeal PB

Loaded PB

Ingredients

- ½ cup butter, softened
- ½ cup crunchy peanut butter
- ½ cup sugar
- ½ cup brown sugar
- 1 egg

- 1 ½ cups flour
- 1 teaspoon baking soda
- ¼ teaspoon salt
- 1 cup Reese's Mini Pieces candies
- ¾ cup dry-roasted peanuts

USE A
9" x 9"
PAN

1. Preheat the oven to 375°F and grease or line a 9" x 9" baking pan; set aside.

2. In a mixing bowl, beat the butter, peanut butter, sugar, brown sugar, and egg until creamy.

3. In a separate bowl, sift together the flour, baking soda, and salt and beat into the butter mixture, a little at a time, until just incorporated.

4. Combine the Reese's Mini Pieces and dry roasted peanuts; set aside ¼ cup of the mixture, stir the remainder into the dough, and spread evenly into prepped pan. Sprinkle the set-aside candy mixture over the top.

5. Bake for 25 to 30 minutes, until it tests done with a toothpick.

6. Let cool on a wire rack before cutting into bars. Enjoy!

Red Velvet Cookie Squares

USE A 9" x 13" PAN

Ingredients

- 2 cups flour, plus 5 tablespoons, divided
- 3 teaspoons vanilla, divided
- 1 cup whole milk
- ⅓ cup unsweetened cocoa powder
- ½ teaspoon salt

- 1 teaspoon baking powder
- ½ teaspoom baking soda
- 1 cup butter, softened
- 2 ½ cups sugar, divided
- 2 eggs

- 1 (1 ounce) bottle red food coloring
- ⅔ cup butter, diced and softened
- 3 ounces cream cheese, softened
- Sugar pearls and/or white sanding sugar, optional

1. Start the frosting first. Combine 5 tablespoons of flour and 1 cup of milk in a saucepan over medium heat; cook, whisking constantly until the mixture thickens and just starts to boil.

2. Remove from the heat, stir in 1 teaspoon of vanilla, and cool slightly. Press plastic wrap directly on the mixture and refrigerate until chilled.

3. Preheat the oven to 350°F. Grease or line a 9" x 13" baking pan and set aside.

4. For the cookie, whisk together 2 cups of flour, cocoa powder, salt, baking powder, and baking soda. In a mixing bowl, beat together the butter and 1 ½ cups of sugar until light and fluffy.

5. Add the eggs, one at a time, mixing until incorporated. Slowly stir in 2 teaspoons of vanilla and food coloring. Add the dry ingredients, a little at a time, until just combined.

6. Press the dough evenly into the prepped pan. Bake for 15 to 20 minutes, until it tests done with a toothpick. Cool in the pan on a wire rack.

7. Finish the frosting by beating together the butter and sugar until light and smooth. Beat in the cream cheese until well combined. Add the chilled milk mixture, a little at a time, beating well after each addition.

8. Continue beating until the frosting resembles whipped cream. Spread the frosting over the cooled cookie and cut into bars. Sprinkle with sugar pearls and/or white sanding sugar if using. Serve and enjoy!

Chocolate Chip Pecan Meringues

USE A 10" x 15" PAN

Ingredients

- 4 egg whites
- 2 egg yolks
- ½ cup butter, softened
- ½ cup sugar
- 1 ½ cups brown sugar, divided

- 3 tablespoons milk
- 1 teaspoon vanilla
- 2 cups flour
- 2 teaspoons baking powder
- 1 teaspoon baking soda

- ½ teaspoon salt
- 1 cup semisweet chocolate chips
- ¾ cup chopped pecans

1. Put egg whites in a small bowl and egg yolks in a big mixing bowl and set both aside at room temperature for 30 minutes. Grease or line a 10" x 15" baking pan and set aside.

2. Preheat the oven to 325°F. To the bowl with the egg yolks, add butter, sugar, and ½ cup of the brown sugar; beat until light and fluffy. Beat in milk and vanilla.

3. In a separate bowl, whisk together the flour, baking powder, baking soda, and salt; gradually beat into the creamed mixture, until just combined. Press evenly into the prepped pan.

4. In a clean mixing bowl with clean beaters, beat the egg whites on medium speed until foamy. Gradually add the remaining 1 cup brown sugar, a little at a time, beating on high after each addition until dissolved. Continue beating until thick and glossy.

5. Fold in the chocolate chips and pecans. Spread evenly over the dough in the pan.

6. Bake on the lowest oven rack for 25 to 30 minutes, until lightly browned. Set the pan on a wire rack to cool then chill for 30 minutes before cutting into bars. Serve and enjoy!

Cookies and Cream Cherry Treats

USE A 9" x 9" PAN

Ingredients

- 1 ½ cups Oreo cookies, crushed and divided
- 2 tablespoons butter or margarine, melted
- 1 cup boiling water
- 2 (6-ounce) packages cherry gelatin
- ⅔ cup chopped maraschino cherries
- ½ cup light corn syrup
- 2 cups whipped topping

1. In a medium bowl, combine 1 cup crushed Oreo cookies and melted butter. Press mixture firmly into bottom of a greased 9" x 9" pan.

2. In a medium bowl, combine boiling water and cherry gelatin. Stir at least 2 minutes, until completely dissolved. Add chopped cherries and corn syrup, stirring until well blended.

3. Refrigerate 30 minutes, until slightly thickened. Pour mixture over crust. Refrigerate for an additional 3 hours until firm.

4. Before serving, spread whipped topping over bars and sprinkle with remaining ½ cup crushed Oreos. Cut into squares before serving.

Chocolate-Covered Crunch Bars

USE A 9" x 9" PAN

Ingredients

- 32 large marshmallows
- ¼ cup butter or margarine
- ½ teaspoon vanilla
- 5 cups Corn Flakes cereal
- 1 cup chocolate chips

1. Grease a 9" x 9" pan and set aside.

2. In a large saucepan over low heat, melt marshmallows and butter, stirring constantly, until mixture is smooth. Remove from heat and stir in vanilla.

3. Stir in half of the Corn Flakes at a time until evenly coated. Press mixture into prepared pan.

4. In a small saucepan over low heat or a double boiler, heat chocolate chips, stirring frequently, until melted. Spread melted chocolate over Corn Flake mixture in pan.

5. Let cool before cutting into 2-inch bars. Serve, crunch, and enjoy!

Lemon Maple Oat Bars

USE A
9" x 13"
PAN

Ingredients

- 1 (8-ounce) package pitted dates, chopped
- ¾ cup water
- ⅓ cup pure maple syrup
- Zest of 1 lemon
- ⅔ cup sugar
- ½ cup butter, softened
- 1 cup flour
- 1 cup old-fashioned oats
- ¼ teaspoon baking soda
- ¼ teaspoon salt

1. Grease or line a 9" x 13" baking pan; set aside.

2. In a heavy saucepan, combine the dates, water, and syrup. Bring to a boil over medium heat; cook for 12 minutes, until most of the liquid is absorbed, stirring often. Stir in lemon zest; let cool for 30 minutes.

3. Preheat the oven to 400°F. In a mixing bowl, beat together the sugar and butter until smooth.

4. In a separate bowl, whisk together the flour, oats, baking soda, and salt; mix slowly into the butter mixture until just combined. Press 2 ½ cups of the mixture into the prepped pan.

5. Put blobs of the date mixture over the top and spread carefully; sprinkle with the remaining crumbly mixture.

6. Bake for 20 to 25 minutes or until golden brown. Cool in the pan on a wire rack before cutting into bars. Enjoy!

Andes Cookie Squares

USE A
9" x 13"
PAN

Ingredients

- 1 cup butter, softened, divided
- 2 ¼ teaspoons vanilla, divided
- ½ cup brown sugar
- ½ cup sugar
- 1 egg
- 2 tablespoons, plus ⅓ cup whipping cream, divided
- 2 cups flour
- ½ cup unsweetened cocoa powder
- 1 teaspoon baking powder
- ¾ teaspoon salt, divided
- ¼ to ½ teaspoon mint flavoring
- 4 cups powdered sugar
- Green gel food coloring, as needed
- 1 (4.67-ounce) package Andes Creme De Menthe Thins, unwrapped and coarsely chopped

1. Preheat the oven to 375°F and line a 9" x 13" baking pan with parchment paper; set aside.

2. To make the cookie, in a mixing bowl, beat ½ cup butter, 2 teaspoons vanilla, brown sugar, sugar, egg, and 2 tablespoons whipping cream until well combined.

3. In a separate bowl, whisk together the flour, cocoa powder, baking powder, and ½ teaspoon salt. Slowly add the dry ingredients to the butter mixture, beating until incorporated.

4. Press the mixture evenly into the prepped pan and bake for 15 minutes or until it tests done with a toothpick. Cool in the pan on a wire rack.

5. For the frosting, beat together ½ cup butter, ¼ teaspoon salt, ¼ teaspoon vanilla, mint flavoring, and ⅓ cup whipping cream.

6. Add the powdered sugar, a little at a time, beating on low speed until well blended; beat on medium speed for about a minute. Beat in enough food coloring to reach the desired shade of green.

7. Spread the frosting over the cooled cookie and cut into bars. Sprinkle the candies evenly over the individual bars. Serve and enjoy!

Caramel Delights

USE A
9" x 9"
PAN

Ingredients

- 2 cups sweetened flaked coconut
- 1 cup flour
- ¼ cup sugar
- ½ cup butter, softened, divided
- ¼ teaspoon vanilla
- 1 teaspoon water
- 25 caramels, unwrapped
- 1 cup semisweet chocolate chips, divided
- 1 teaspoon shortening, divided

1. Toast coconut in a dry skillet over medium heat for 10 to 15 minutes or until lightly browned, stirring occasionally; let cool.

2. Preheat the oven to 350°F and line a 9" x 9" baking pan with parchment paper; set aside.

3. Mix the flour, sugar, 6 tablespoons of the butter, vanilla, and 1 teaspoon water in a bowl until ingredients come together into a ball. Press into the prepped pan and bake for 15 minutes, until edges are lightly browned. Set the pan on a wire rack to cool.

4. In a small saucepan over low heat, combine the caramels, 2 tablespoons water, and the remaining 2 tablespoons butter, stirring until melted.

5. Add 1 ½ cups of the toasted coconut and stir well. Spread evenly over the cooled cookie. Sprinkle with the remaining ½ cup coconut and press into the caramel. Let cool for an hour.

6. Lift parchment paper to remove from pan and cut into bars.

7. Melt ¾ cup of the chocolate chips with ¾ teaspoon of the shortening in the microwave on high, stirring every 15 seconds until smooth. Spread about 1 teaspoon chocolate over the bottom of each bar and set on parchment paper to dry.

8. Melt the remaining ¼ cup chocolate chips with the remaining ¼ teaspoon shortening and drizzle over the tops of the bars. Once cooled, serve and enjoy!

3 Cake Mix Cookie Bars

Toffee

Ingredients

- 6 tablespoons butter
- 1 (15- to 16-ounce) yellow cake mix
- 1 egg
- 1 ½ (8-ounce) packages chocolate toffee bits
- 1 (14-ounce) can sweetened condensed milk

1. Preheat the oven to 350°F and grease or line a 9" x 13" baking pan; set aside.
2. Melt the butter and cool slightly.
3. Combine the cake mix, egg, and the melted butter. Press evenly into the prepped pan.
4. Sprinkle the chocolate toffee bits over the top and drizzle the sweetened condensed milk evenly over the bits.
5. Bake for 25 to 30 minutes or until set. Cool completely before cutting into bars. Enjoy!

Coconut Fudge

Ingredients

- 1 (16- to 18-ounce) chocolate cake mix
- 3 tablespoons vegetable oil
- ¼ cup plain low-fat yogurt
- 2 eggs
- ½ cup sweetened flaked coconut
- ¼ cup white baking chips, plus more for sprinkling
- ¼ cup semisweet chocolate chips, plus more for sprinkling

1. Preheat the oven to 350°F and grease or line a 9" x 13" baking pan; set aside.
2. In a big bowl, stir together the cake mix, vegetable oil, yogurt, and eggs until well blended.
3. Stir in the coconut, white baking chips, and semisweet chocolate chips and spread evenly into the prepped pan.
4. Sprinkle some white and semisweet chips over the top. Bake for 25 minutes or until set. Cool completely before cutting into bars. Enjoy!

Carrot

Toffee

Coconut
Fudge

Carrot

Ingredients

- 1 (15- to 16-ounce) carrot cake mix
- ⅓ cup vegetable oil
- 2 eggs
- ½ cup softened butter
- 1 (8-ounce) package cream cheese, softened
- 1 teaspoon vanilla
- 4 cups powdered sugar, sifted
- ¼ teaspoon salt
- Orange decorating sprinkles or sanding sugar, for decorating

USE A
9" x 13"
PAN

1. Preheat the oven to 350°F and grease or line a 9" x 13" baking pan; set aside.

2. In a big bowl, stir together the cake mix, vegetable oil, and eggs until well combined. Spread the batter evenly into the prepped pan.

3. Bake for 18 to 20 minutes, or until it tests done with a toothpick. Cool completely.

4. For the cream cheese frosting, beat together the butter, cream cheese, and vanilla until smooth. Gradually beat in powdered sugar and salt. Spread evenly over the cooled cookie before cutting into bars.

5. Sprinkle with orange decorating sprinkles or sanding sugar if you'd like. Enjoy!

Mixed Berry Tarts

USE A 10"x15" PAN

Ingredients

- ½ cup butter, softened
- ½ cup sugar
- 1 egg
- ½ teaspoon baking soda
- ½ teaspoon white distilled vinegar
- 2 cups plus 2 tablespoons flour
- 1 cup mixed berry preserves, room temperature
- Powdered sugar, for topping

1. In a mixing bowl, cream together the butter, sugar, and egg. In a cup or small bowl, mix the baking soda and vinegar; immediately add to the creamed mixture and beat until well combined. Slowly beat in the flour until just incorporated.

2. Roll one-third of the dough into a ball and place in the freezer for about an hour.

3. Place the remaining two-thirds of the dough onto a big sheet of parchment paper; sprinkle lightly with flour, and roll out to 9" x 13".

4. Transfer the dough and parchment paper to 10" x 15" baking pan (or any size larger than 9" x 13"). Cover with plastic wrap and set aside until the dough in the freezer is thoroughly chilled.

5. Preheat the oven to 350°F. Spread the preserves evenly over the rolled-out dough.

6. Grate or finely chop the chilled dough evenly over the top to cover most of the preserves. Bake for 25 to 30 minutes or until golden brown.

7. Cool in the pan on a wire rack before dusting with powdered sugar and cutting into bars. Serve and enjoy!

Cherry-Almond Bars

Ingredients

- 1 (16-ounce) jar maraschino cherries
- ¾ cup butter, softened
- 1 cup sugar
- 2 eggs
- ¾ teaspoon almond extract, divided
- 2 ½ cups flour

- ½ teaspoon baking powder
- ½ teaspoon salt
- 1 cup powdered sugar
- 1 tablespoon butter, melted
- 1 to 2 teaspoons whipping cream

USE A
9" x 13"
PAN

1. Preheat the oven to 375°F and grease or line a 9" x 13" baking pan; set aside.

2. To make the cookie, drain the maraschino cherries, setting aside 2 tablespoons of the juice for the cherry drizzle. Coarsely chop the cherries, rinse well, and set aside.

3. Cream together the butter and sugar until fluffy. Add the eggs, one at a time, mixing well after each addition. Mix in ½ teaspoon almond extract.

4. In a separate bowl, whisk together the flour, baking powder, and salt and slowly add to the creamed mixture, beating until just incorporated. Fold in the set-aside cherries.

5. Press the dough into the prepped pan and bake for 20 to 23 minutes, until golden brown and a toothpick comes out with a few crumbs remaining. Cool in the pan on a wire rack.

6. For the cherry drizzle, stir together the powdered sugar, reserved cherry syrup, butter, ¼ teaspoon almond extract, and whipping cream until smooth; drizzle over the cooled cookie and cut into bars. Serve and enjoy the sweetness!

3 Snickerdoodle Bars

Basic Snickerdoodles

Ingredients

- 1 cup softened butter
- 2 cups, plus 2 tablespoons sugar, divided
- ½ teaspoon salt
- 2 eggs
- 1 tablespoon vanilla
- 2 cups flour
- 2 teaspoons cinnamon

1. Preheat the oven to 350°F; grease or line a 9" x 13" baking pan and set aside.

2. In a mixing bowl, cream together the butter and 2 cups of sugar until light and fluffy.

3. Beat in the salt, eggs, and vanilla. Add the flour, a little at a time, until just incorporated.

4. Spread the dough evenly into the prepped pan. Stir together 2 tablespoons sugar and cinnamon and sprinkle over the dough.

5. Bake for 30 to 40 minutes until set in the middle. Cool completely before cutting into bars. Enjoy!

Caramel Doodles

Ingredients

- 1 cup butter, softened
- 2 cups brown sugar
- 2 eggs
- 2 teaspoons vanilla
- 2 ½ cups flour
- 2 teaspoons baking powder
- 1 teaspoon salt
- ¼ cup sugar
- 1 tablespoon cinnamon
- 1 (10-ounce) bag caramels, unwrapped
- ¼ cup , plus 1 ½ tablespoons whipping cream, divided
- 1 (4-ounce) package white baking chocolate, chopped
- 1 teaspoon light corn syrup

1. Preheat the oven to 350°F. Grease or line a 9" x 13" baking pan; set aside.

2. In a mixing bowl, beat the butter with brown sugar until light and fluffy. Beat in eggs and vanilla.

3. Whisk together the flour, baking powder, and salt; gradually beat into the creamed mixture. Press evenly into the prepped pan.

4. Mix the sugar and cinnamon; set aside 2 tablespoons and sprinkle the remainder over the dough. Bake for 25 to 30 minutes, until edges are light brown. Cool completely.

5. In a double boiler, melt together the caramels and ¼ cup whipping cream, stirring often; spread over the cooled cookie.

6. Melt together the white baking chocolate, 1 ½ tablespoons whipping cream, and the light corn syrup, stirring constantly; drizzle over the caramel and sprinkle with set-aside cinnamon-sugar. Chill before cutting into bars. Enjoy!

Basic Snickerdoodles

Frosted Doodles

Caramel Doodles

Frosted Doodles

Ingredients

- 1 ½ cups softened butter, divided
- 1 ¼ cups, plus 1 tablespoon sugar, divided
- ½ cup brown sugar
- 2 teaspoons vanilla, divided
- 3 eggs
- 2 ⅓ cups flour
- 1 ¼ teaspoon baking powder
- ½ teaspoon salt
- 2 teaspoons cinnamon, divided
- 1 ½ cups powdered sugar
- 1 tablespoon milk

USE A
9" x 13"
PAN

1. Preheat the oven to 350°F. Grease or line a 9" x 13" baking pan; set aside.

2. In a mixing bowl, beat ¾ cup softened butter, 1 ¼ cups sugar, brown sugar, and 1 teaspoon vanilla until creamy. Beat in the eggs, one at a time, until incorporated.

3. In a separate bowl, whisk together the flour, baking powder, and salt; beat into the butter mixture, a little at a time until just combined. Press half the batter into the prepped pan.

4. Stir together 1 tablespoon sugar and 1 teaspoon cinnamon and sprinkle over the dough. Drop teaspoon-sized blobs of the remaining dough close together over the top to nearly cover the cinnamon-sugar; spread carefully.

5. Bake for 25 minutes or until golden brown. Cool completely.

6. For the cinnamon-sugar frosting: Beat ¾ cup of the softened butter, the powdered sugar, 1 teaspoon cinnamon, the milk, and 1 teaspoon vanilla; spread over the cooled cookie. Cut into bars and enjoy!

Mississippi Mud Bars

USE A 10" x 15" PAN

Ingredients

- 1 ½ cups butter, divided
- ⅔ cup semisweet chocolate chips
- 2 cups sugar
- 1 ½ cups flour
- ½ cup, plus ⅓ cup unsweetened cocoa powder, divided
- ¾ teaspoon salt
- 4 eggs
- 2 teaspoons vanilla, divided
- 1 (10.5-ounce) package mini marshmallows
- 1 cup chopped pecans
- ⅓ cup milk
- 3 ¼ cups powdered sugar, sifted

1. Preheat the oven to 350°F. Grease or line a 10" x 15" baking pan and set aside.

2. To make the cookie, in a big microwave-safe bowl, combine 1 cup butter and chocolate chips and microwave for 1 to 2 minutes, stirring every 30 seconds until smooth.

3. Whisk in the sugar, flour, ½ cup cocoa powder, salt, eggs, and 1 teaspoon vanilla until blended. Spread the mixture into the prepped pan and bake for 20 minutes.

4. Immediately sprinkle the marshmallows on top. Bake for 8 to 12 minutes longer, until golden brown.

5. Meanwhile, for the glaze, toast the pecans by tossing them in a single layer on a baking sheet and bake for 10 minutes until golden brown, stirring occasionally; set aside.

6. Melt ½ cup butter in a medium saucepan over medium-low heat. Whisk in ⅓ cup cocoa powder, milk, and 1 teaspoon vanilla; heat for 1 minute.

7. Whisk in the powdered sugar until smooth. Drizzle the glaze over the warm cookie and sprinkle with the toasted pecans. Cool in the pan on a wire rack then chill before cutting into bars. Enjoy!

Peanut Butter Èclair

USE A 10"x15" PAN

Ingredients

- 1 cup sugar
- 1 cup light corn syrup
- 2 cups crunchy peanut butter
- 8 cups Frosted Flakes cereal
- 1 ¼ cups butter, divided
- 4 cups powdered sugar
- 2 (3.4-ounce) packages vanilla instant pudding mix
- ⅓ cup plus 1 tablespoon milk
- 2 cups semisweet chocolate chips

1. Grease or line a 10" x 15" baking pan and set aside.

2. In a big saucepan, combine the sugar and syrup. Bring to a boil and boil for 1 minute, stirring occasionally.

3. Remove the pan from the heat and stir in the peanut butter. Add the cereal, stirring until well coated. Press evenly into the prepped pan.

4. In a medium microwave-safe bowl, melt ¾ cup of the butter in the microwave. Stir in the powdered sugar and both pudding packages. Slowly stir in the milk, until smooth and thick; spread evenly over the cookie layer.

5. Melt together the chocolate chips and the remaining ½ cup butter; spread over the pudding layer and chill before cutting into bars. Enjoy!

Nutty Bars

USE A 10" x 15" PAN

Ingredients

- 12 graham crackers
- ¾ cup brown sugar
- ¾ cup butter
- 1 cup chocolate chips
- 1 cup salted peanuts

1. Line a 10" x 15" jellyroll pan with graham crackers.

2. In a large saucepan over medium heat, combine brown sugar and butter. Cook until mixture comes to a full boil.

3. Boil for 5 minutes, stirring constantly. Immediately pour over graham crackers in pan and spread evenly.

4. Sprinkle with chocolate chips and let stand for 1 minute. Sprinkle with peanuts and lightly press into chocolate.

5. Let cool completely before cutting or breaking into squares. Enjoy!

Chocolate Creamsicle Bars

USE A 9" x 9" PAN

Ingredients

- 1 ¼ cups chocolate wafer cookies, finely crushed
- ⅔ cup plus 1 tablespoon butter, melted, divided
- 1 ½ cups powdered sugar
- 2 teaspoons orange peel, grated
- 1 tablespoon milk
- ½ teaspoon vanilla
- 1 tablespoon cocoa powder

1. In a medium bowl, combine crushed chocolate wafer cookies and ⅓ cup melted butter.

2. Press mixture onto the bottom of a greased 9" x 9" pan. Cover and refrigerate for 1 hour, until firm.

3. In a medium mixing bowl, combine powdered sugar, ⅓ cup melted butter, grated orange peel, milk, and vanilla.

4. Beat at medium speed for 3 to 4 minutes, until creamy. Spread mixture over cooled crust.

5. In a separate small bowl, combine remaining 1 tablespoon melted butter and cocoa powder. Drizzle over ingredients in pan.

6. Refrigerate for 1 to 2 hours, until firm, before cutting into bars. Enjoy!

Nuts About Nuts

USE A 9" x 13" PAN

Ingredients

- ½ cup butter, melted
- 1 ½ cups graham cracker crumbs
- 1 (14-ounce) can sweetened condensed milk
- 1 cup ricotta cheese
- 1 teaspoon orange zest
- 1 teaspoon cinnamon
- 1 (10-ounce) package mini chocolate chips
- ½ cup salted pistachios, shelled and coarsely chopped
- ½ cup salted pepitas (pumpkin seed kernels)
- Powdered sugar, for dusting, optional

1. Preheat the oven to 350°F. Grease or line a 9" x 13" baking pan; if lining, grease the liner. Set aside.

2. Stir together the butter and cracker crumbs; press into the prepped pan. In a medium bowl, stir together the sweetened condensed milk, ricotta cheese, orange zest, and cinnamon; pour onto the crust.

3. Sprinkle the chocolate chips, pistachios, and pepitas evenly over the top, pressing to adhere. Bake for 25 to 30 minutes, until the edges are lightly browned.

4. Cool in the pan on a wire rack then chill thoroughly before cutting into bars. Dust with powdered sugar if you'd like. Keep refrigerated until serving. Enjoy!

M&M Crunch

USE A 9" x 13" PAN

Ingredients

- 4 cups corn Chex cereal
- 1 cup salted peanuts
- 1 cup M&M candies
- ½ cup butter
- 1 cup brown sugar
- ½ cup light corn syrup
- 2 tablespoons flour

1. In a large bowl, combine cereal, peanuts, and M&Ms and set aside.

2. In a large saucepan over low heat, melt butter. Stir in brown sugar, corn syrup, and flour.

3. Increase heat to medium and cook mixture, stirring occasionally, until mixture comes to a full boil. Boil for 1 minute and pour over cereal in bowl.

4. Stir until well coated and press into the bottom of a greased 9" x 13" pan. Let cool completely before cutting into bars. Enjoy!

Java Pudding Squares

USE A 9" x 13" PAN

Ingredients

- 15 chocolate graham crackers, divided
- 2 (8-ounce) packages cream cheese, softened
- 3 ½ cups milk, divided
- 3 (5.9-ounce) packages instant chocolate pudding mix
- 1 tablespoon instant coffee
- ¼ teaspoon cinnamon
- 1 (8-ounce) container whipped topping, divided
- 1 (1-ounce) square semisweet chocolate, grated

1. Place half of the chocolate graham crackers onto the bottom of a greased 9" x 13" pan, cutting crackers to fit, if necessary.

2. In a large mixing bowl, beat softened cream cheese at low speed until smooth. Gradually beat in 1 cup milk. Add remaining milk, chocolate pudding mixes, instant coffee, and cinnamon.

3. Beat 1 to 2 minutes, until mixture thickens. Gently stir in the whipped topping.

4. Spread half of the pudding mixture over graham crackers in pan. Arrange remaining half of graham crackers over pudding layer. Top with remaining pudding mixture and cover with remaining whipped topping. Sprinkle with grated chocolate.

5. Freeze for 3 hours or overnight before cutting into bars and serving.

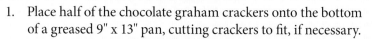

Berry Popcorn Bars

Ingredients

USE A 9" x 13" PAN

- 2 cups flour
- ¼ teaspoon salt
- ½ cup powdered sugar
- 1 cup cold butter, cubed
- 1 egg white, lightly beaten
- 1 (12-ounce) jar strawberry preserves
- 4 cups popcorn, popped
- ¼ cup dark chocolate chips

1. Preheat the oven to 350°F and grease or line a 9" x 13" baking pan; set aside.

2. Put the flour, salt, and powdered sugar into a food processor; pulse to combine. Add the butter and process until pieces are the size of peas; press evenly into the prepped pan.

3. Brush the egg white over the cookie crust and bake for 25 minutes, until golden brown.

4. Remove from the oven and immediately spread the strawberry preserves over the crust. Press the popcorn into the preserves and set aside to cool.

5. Melt the dark chocolate chips and drizzle over the top. Set aside until the chocolate has cooled before cutting into bars. Enjoy!

Patchwork Cookie Bars

USE A 13" x 18" PAN

Ingredients

- 1 ½ cups butter, softened
- 1 cup sugar
- 1 cup brown sugar
- 2 eggs
- 1 teaspoon vanilla
- 3 cups flour
- 1 teaspoon baking soda
- ½ teaspoon salt

Snickerdoodle

- 2 tablespoons sugar + ½ teaspoon cinnamon

Double Chocolate

- 2 tablespoons cocoa powder + ¼ cup dark chocolate chips

Macadamia Nut

- ¼ cup chopped macadamia nuts + ¼ cup white baking chips

Oatmeal Raisin

- ⅓ cup oats + ¼ cup raisins + ¼ teaspoon cinnamon

Peanut Butter

- ⅓ cup creamy peanut butter

Chocolate Chip

- ½ cup milk chocolate chips

1. Preheat the oven to 350°F and grease a 13" x 18" baking pan; set aside.

2. In a big mixing bowl, beat the butter, sugar, and brown sugar until well combined. Beat in the eggs and vanilla.

3. In a small bowl, whisk together the flour, baking soda, and salt and beat into butter mixture on low speed until just incorporated. Divide the dough evenly among six small bowls (about ¾ cup dough in each).

4. To each bowl, stir in the ingredients for the individual flavors listed above.

5. Press the cookie dough evenly into the prepped pan in a grid pattern, forming six squares, sides touching and filling the pan. Bake for 20 minutes or until done.

6. Let cool before cutting into bars. Serve, mix and match, and enjoy!

Snickerdoodle

Oatmeal Raisin

Double Chocolate

Peanut Butter

Chocolate Chip

Macadamia Nut

Snickering Cookie Bars

USE A 9" x 9" PAN

Ingredients

- ⅔ cup butter, softened
- ¼ cup sugar
- 1 ¼ cups flour
- ¼ teaspoon salt
- 1 teaspoon vanilla
- 1 (11-ounce) bag caramels, unwrapped
- ¼ cup heavy cream
- 1 cup dry-roasted peanuts
- 1 (11.5-ounce) package milk chocolate chips

1. Preheat the oven to 350°F and line a 9" x 9" baking pan with parchment paper, allowing some to hang over sides of pan; set aside.

2. In a medium mixing bowl, beat the butter on medium speed until creamy. Beat in the sugar, flour, salt, and vanilla until well mixed and crumbly. Press into the prepped pan and bake about 20 minutes or until lightly browned. Let cool.

3. Combine the caramels and cream in the microwave on high for 30 seconds at a time, stirring until smooth. Stir in the peanuts and spread the mixture evenly over the crust; let cool at least 10 minutes.

4. In a clean microwaveable bowl, melt the chocolate chips in the microwave for 30 seconds at a time, stirring until smooth. Pour the chocolate over the caramel layer and spread evenly. Let cool about 3 hours or until chocolate looks dry.

5. Lift parchment paper to remove from pan and cut into bars. (You can pop the pan into the freezer for 5 minutes first to make cutting easy.) Serve and enjoy!

With the crunchy goodness of a cookie and the sweet toppings of a candy bar, these treats will earn two thumbs up every time!

3 No-Bake Cookie Bars

Peanut Butter

Ingredients

- 1 cup butter
- ½ cup brown sugar
- 1 teaspoon vanilla
- 3 cups gluten-free oats
- 1 cup milk chocolate chips
- ½ cup creamy peanut butter

USE AN 8" x 8" PAN

1. Grease or line an 8" x 8" pan and set aside.

2. In a big saucepan, melt the butter over medium heat. Stir in the brown sugar and vanilla until brown sugar is dissolved.

3. Stir in the oats and cook over low heat for 2 to 3 minutes. Press half the mixture into the prepped pan; set the remaining mixture aside.

4. Melt together the chocolate chips and peanut butter, stirring until smooth; pour over the mixture in the pan, spreading evenly. Crumble the set-aside oatmeal mixture over the chocolate, pressing gently.

5. Refrigerate a few hours before cutting into bars. Serve and enjoy!

Coconut-Walnut

Ingredients

- 1 cup butter
- 2 cups sugar
- ½ cup milk
- 1 cup semisweet chocolate chips
- ¾ cup sweetened flaked coconut
- ½ cup chopped walnuts
- 3 cups gluten-free oats
- 1 teaspoon vanilla

USE A 9" x 13" PAN

1. Grease or line a 9" x 13" pan and set aside.

2. In a big saucepan, combine the butter, sugar, and milk over medium-high heat, stirring often. Bring to a boil and boil for 1 minute.

3. Remove from the heat and add the semisweet chocolate chips, stirring until melted.

4. Stir in the coconut, walnuts, oats, and vanilla until incorporated. Dump mixture into prepped pan and smooth evenly.

5. Cool completely before cutting into bars. Serve and enjoy!

eanut
3utter

coconut-
walnut

Cookie
Dough

Cookie Dough

Ingredients

- ½ cup butter, softened
- ¼ cup brown sugar
- ½ cup powdered sugar
- 1 teaspoon vanilla
- 2 cups flour

- 1 (14-ounce) can sweetened condensed milk
- 1½ cups mini chocolate chips, plus more for sprinkling
- ¾ cup semisweet chocolate chips
- ¾ cup milk chocolate chips

USE A
9" x 9"
PAN

1. Grease or line a 9" x 9" pan and set aside.

2. In a mixing bowl, beat together the butter, brown sugar, powdered sugar, and vanilla until light and fluffy.

3. Gradually beat in the flour, a little at a time, alternately with the sweetened condensed milk, until well blended. Stir in the mini chocolate chips.

4. Press the dough into the prepped pan. Refrigerate several hours, until firm.

5. Melt together the semisweet and milk chocolate chips and spread evenly over the chilled cookie dough. Sprinkle with a handful of mini chocolate chips and chill for an hour before cutting into bars. Yum!

If eating uncooked flour concerns you, use oat flour instead. To make it yourself, blend 2⅔ cups old-fashioned oats (measures 2 cups after blending) in a high-powered blender until it becomes the texture of flour.

Rice Krispies Squares

USE A 9" x 13" PAN

GLUTEN FREE

Ingredients

- 1 cup corn syrup
- 1 cup sugar
- 1 cup peanut butter
- 6 cups Rice Krispies cereal
- 1 cup chocolate chips
- 1 cup butterscotch chips

1. Grease a 9" x 13" pan and set aside.

2. In a large saucepan over medium heat, combine corn syrup and sugar until mixture begins to boil. Remove from heat.

3. Stir in peanut butter and Rice Krispies. Press mixture into greased pan.

4. In a microwave or double boiler over simmering water, melt chocolate chips and butterscotch chips, stirring often until smooth. Spread melted chocolate over cereal mixture.

5. Cool in refrigerator until firm, about 15 minutes. Cut into squares, serve, and enjoy!

Milky Way Krispie Clouds

GLUTEN FREE

USE A 7" x 11" PAN

Ingredients

- 4 (2.05-ounce) Milky Way bars
- ¾ cups butter or margarine, divided
- 3 cups Rice Krispies cereal
- 1 cup milk chocolate chips

1. In microwave or a double boiler, melt candy bars and ½ cup butter, stirring occasionally, until smooth.

2. Stir in cereal until well coated. Press mixture into a greased 7" x 11" pan.

3. In a separate microwave-safe bowl or double boiler, melt chocolate chips and remaining ¼ cup butter, stirring until smooth. Remove from heat and spread chocolate mixture over ingredients in pan.

4. Refrigerate 1 hour, or until firm, before cutting into squares and serving.

Golden S'more Squares

USE A
9" x 13"
PAN

Ingredients

- ¾ cup light corn syrup
- 3 tablespoons butter
- 1 teaspoon vanilla
- 1 (11.5-ounce) package milk chocolate chips
- 9 cups or 1 (12-ounce) package Golden Grahams cereal
- 3 cups miniature marshmallows

1. Grease a 9" x 13" pan and set aside.

2. In a medium saucepan over medium heat, combine corn syrup, butter, vanilla, and milk chocolate chips, stirring constantly, until boiling.

3. In a large bowl, place Golden Grahams cereal. Pour chocolate mixture over Golden Grahams cereal and toss until well coated. Fold in marshmallows.

4. Spread mixture into greased pan. Let stand for 1 hour.

5. Once cooled, cut into squares, serve, and enjoy!

Peanut Butter Crunch Bars

Ingredients

- 1 (14-ounce) can sweetened condensed milk
- 1 (10-ounce) package Reese's peanut butter chips
- 3 cups miniature marshmallows
- 1 (16-ounce) jar salted or dry roasted peanuts, divided

USE A 9" x 13" PAN

1. In a microwave-safe bowl, combine sweetened condensed milk, peanut butter chips, and marshmallows. Microwave for about 2½ minutes, stirring often, until melted.

2. Spread half of the peanuts into a greased 9" x 13" pan.

3. Spread marshmallow mixture over peanuts. Top with remaining peanuts.

4. Refrigerate for 1 hour before cutting into bars. Store at room temperature. Enjoy!

Cereal Squares

Ingredients

- 1 cup white corn syrup
- 1 ¾ cups sugar, divided
- 1 cup peanut butter
- 6 cups Special K cereal
- 3 tablespoons butter or margarine
- 3 tablespoons milk
- ½ cup chocolate chips

USE AN 11" x 14" PAN

1. In a large saucepan, combine white corn syrup and 1 cup of sugar. Bring to a boil and add peanut butter.

2. Stir in Special K cereal and transfer to a greased 11" x 14" pan.

3. In a separate bowl, combine butter, milk, and remaining ¾ cup sugar. Bring to a boil, stirring constantly, and add chocolate chips. Mix well until smooth.

4. Pour over ingredients in pan. Let cool and cut into squares. Enjoy!

Easy 4-Layer Choco Bars

USE A 9" x 13" PAN

Ingredients

- 1 (16-ounce) package Club crackers
- 1 cup graham cracker crumbs
- ¾ cup brown sugar
- ½ cup sugar
- ⅓ cup milk
- ½ cup margarine
- ⅔ cup peanut butter
- 1 cup chocolate chips

1. Place 1 layer of Club crackers on the bottom of a greased 9" x 13" pan. Set aside.

2. In a large saucepan over low heat, combine graham cracker crumbs, brown sugar, sugar, milk, and margarine. Let boil for 5 minutes.

3. Pour mixture over crackers in pan. Cover with another layer of Club crackers.

4. In a microwave or double boiler, melt peanut butter and chocolate chips, stirring often until smooth. Pour melted chocolate mixture over top layer of Club crackers.

5. Refrigerate and cut into bars once cooled. Serve and enjoy!

Simple Rocky Road No-Bakes

USE A 9″ x 9″ PAN

Ingredients

- 2 cups dark chocolate chips
- 1 cup peanut butter
- 4 cups miniature marshmallows

1. Grease a 9" x 9" pan and set aside.

2. In a medium saucepan over low heat, melt the chocolate chips and peanut butter, stirring, until completely melted.

3. Remove from heat and stir in marshmallows. Pour mixture into prepared pan.

4. Let cool in refrigerator before cutting into squares and serving.

Puffed and Crunched Bars

USE A 9″ x 9″ PAN

Ingredients

- 8 cups puffed wheat cereal
- 3 tablespoons cocoa powder
- ⅓ cup corn syrup
- ¼ cup brown sugar
- ⅓ cup butter or margarine

1. Grease a 9" x 9" pan and set aside.

2. In a large bowl, place puffed wheat cereal and set aside.

3. Grease the rim of a medium saucepan to prevent boil-over. In the saucepan, combine the cocoa powder, corn syrup, brown sugar, and butter.

4. Cook over medium heat, stirring often, until mixture comes to a full boil. Allow to boil for 1 minute before removing from heat. Pour chocolate mixture over puffed wheat and stir until evenly coated.

5. Using a greased spatula, press mixture into the prepared pan. Allow to cool before cutting into squares and serving. Yum!

Cheery Honey Nut Squares

USE A 9" x 13" PAN

GLUTEN FREE

Ingredients

- ½ cup sugar
- ½ cup honey
- ½ cup peanut butter
- 3 cups Cheerios cereal
- 1 cup salted peanuts, optional

1. Grease a 9" x 13" pan and set aside.

2. In a large saucepan over medium heat, stir together sugar and honey. Bring to a boil and remove from heat.

3. Stir in peanut butter until well blended. Add cereal and peanuts (if using) and mix well.

4. Press into prepared pan. Allow to cool and harden before cutting into bars. Enjoy!

Coconut Fudge No-Bakes

USE A 9" x 13" PAN

Ingredients

- 1 cup butter or margarine, melted, divided
- 14 graham crackers, finely crushed
- 1 cup sugar
- 1 (5-ounce) can evaporated milk
- 1 (10.5-ounce) package miniature marshmallows
- 2 cups or 1 (12-ounce) package dark chocolate chunks
- 1 cup chopped walnuts
- 1 cup shredded coconut, toasted

1. In a medium bowl, combine ¾ cup melted butter and graham cracker crumbs. Press mixture onto bottom of a foil-lined 9" x 13" pan and set aside.

2. In a large saucepan over medium heat, combine remaining ¼ cup melted butter, sugar, evaporated milk, and marshmallows. Boil for 5 minutes, stirring constantly.

3. Add chocolate and heat until completely melted, stirring constantly. Pour mixture immediately over crust and spread evenly. Sprinkle top with chopped walnuts and toasted coconut, pressing them lightly into the chocolate. Refrigerate for 2 hours before cutting into bars and serving. Yum!

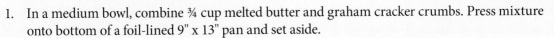

Mini Caramel Krispies

Ingredients

- 3 tablespoons butter or margarine
- 1 (10.5-ounce) package miniature marshmallows
- ½ cup caramel topping
- 6 cups Rice Krispies cereal

1. In a large saucepan over low heat, melt butter. Add marshmallows and stir until completely melted. Remove from heat.

2. Add caramel topping and stir until well combined. Add Rice Krispies cereal, stirring until completely coated.

3. Using a greased spatula, press mixture evenly into a greased 9" x 13" pan. Let cool before cutting into 2-inch squares. Serve immediately.

H.O.P.P. Bars

Ingredients

- 1 ½ cups quick oats
- ½ cup honey
- ½ cup wheat germ
- ½ cup crunchy peanut butter
- ½ cup chopped peanuts

1. In a medium bowl, combine the quick-cooking oats, honey, wheat germ, crunchy peanut butter, and chopped peanuts. Mix thoroughly, until well combined.

2. Shape mixture into a long rectangle and wrap in waxed paper. Chill in refrigerator until hardened.

3. Cut into 1-inch-thick bars and serve. Enjoy!

S'mores Bars

USE A
9" x 13"
PAN

Ingredients

- 7 graham crackers
- 2 ½ cups miniature marshmallows, plus more for topping
- 1 (12-ounce) package chocolate chips
- ⅔ cup light corn syrup
- 3 tablespoons butter or margarine

- ½ cup crunchy peanut butter
- 3 cups Rice Krispies cereal
- Peanuts, chopped, for topping
- Chocolate drizzle, for topping

1. Grease a 9" x 13" microwave-safe pan.

2. Place 6 graham crackers in a single layer on the bottom of the pan. Cut remaining graham cracker to fit in remainder of bottom.

3. Sprinkle marshmallows evenly over graham crackers. Microwave on high for 1 minute, until marshmallows are puffy. Remove from microwave and let cool completely.

4. In a large microwave-safe mixing bowl, combine chocolate chips, corn syrup, and butter. Microwave on high for 1 ½ minutes or until chocolate can be stirred smooth.

5. Stir in peanut butter and add Rice Krispies cereal. Mix until well combined.

6. Spread mixture evenly over marshmallows in pan. Top with mini marshmallows, peanuts, chocolate drizzle, and whatever else you'd like. Cover and refrigerate for 1 hour, until firm.

7. Cut into bars and store in an airtight container in refrigerator. Enjoy!

Strawberries and Cream No-Bakes

GLUTEN FREE

USE A 9"x13" PAN

Ingredients

- 1 ¼ cups pretzels, crushed
- ¼ cup butter or margarine, melted
- 1 (14-ounce) can sweetened condensed milk
- 1 cup pureed strawberries
- ½ cup lime juice
- 1 (8-ounce) container whipped topping
- Fresh sliced strawberries, for topping

1. In a 9" x 13" pan, mix crushed pretzels and melted butter. Press crumb mixture firmly into the bottom of the pan and chill in refrigerator while preparing filling.

2. In a large bowl, combine sweetened condensed milk, pureed strawberries, and lime juice until well blended. Gently fold in whipped topping and pour mixture into chilled crust. Top generously with strawberries.

3. Freeze 6 hours or overnight. Let stand at room temperature for 15 minutes before cutting to serve. Enjoy!

Crème-y Peanut Butter Squares

USE A 9"x9" PAN

Ingredients

- 1 cup marshmallow crème
- 1 cup chunky peanut butter
- 36 Ritz crackers, finely crushed
- ½ cup miniature chocolate chips
- 2 (1-ounce) squares semisweet chocolate, melted

1. In a medium bowl, combine marshmallow crème and peanut butter. Stir in crushed Ritz crackers and chocolate chips.

2. Lightly press mixture into a greased 9" x 9" baking pan. Spread melted chocolate on top.

3. Let stand at room temperature for 30 minutes, until set, before cutting into squares. Serve and enjoy!

Chocolate-Almond Delights

USE A 9" x 13" PAN

Ingredients

- 4 cups powdered sugar
- 1½ cups graham crackers, crushed
- 1½ cups peanut butter
- 1½ cups almonds, chopped and divided
- ¾ cup, plus 3 tablespoons butter or margarine, melted and divided
- 48 caramels, unwrapped
- 1 cup dark chocolate chunks

1. In a large bowl, combine powdered sugar, crushed graham crackers, peanut butter, 1 cup chopped almonds, and ¾ cup melted butter. Mix well and press mixture into a greased 9" x 13" pan.

2. In a large saucepan over low heat, melt caramels in ¼ cup water, stirring frequently until mixture is melted and smooth. Pour over crust.

3. In a separate large saucepan over low heat, melt chocolate and remaining 3 tablespoons butter, stirring often until melted and smooth.

4. Spread mixture over caramel layer. Immediately sprinkle remaining ½ cup chopped almonds over all and gently press into topping. Refrigerate at least 1 hour before cutting into squares and serving.

Chocolatey Walnut Crunch

USE A 9" x 9" PAN

Ingredients

- 2 ½ cups graham crackers, finely crushed
- 2 cups miniature marshmallows
- 1 cup chopped walnuts, plus more for garnish
- 1 cup chocolate chips
- 1 cup evaporated milk
- ½ cup light corn syrup
- ¼ teaspoon salt
- 1 tablespoon butter or margarine
- 1 tablespoon vanilla

1. In a large bowl, combine the crushed graham crackers, marshmallows, and chopped walnuts. Set aside.

2. In a 2-quart saucepan over low heat, combine chocolate chips, evaporated milk, corn syrup, and salt.

3. Heat to a rapid boil for 10 minutes, stirring constantly. Remove from heat and stir in butter and vanilla. Immediately stir chocolate mixture into crumb mixture.

4. Spread all into a greased 9" x 9" pan. Refrigerate for approximately 3 hours, until set, before cutting into squares and serving.

Coconut Cream Cheese Crunch Bars

USE A 10" x 15" PAN

Ingredients

- 1 cup butter or margarine, divided
- 1 cup chocolate chips, divided
- 1 ¾ cups graham crackers, crushed
- 1 cup shredded coconut
- ½ cup walnuts, chopped
- 1 (8-ounce) package cream cheese, softened
- ½ cup sugar
- 1 teaspoon vanilla

1. In a large saucepan over low heat, melt ¾ cup butter and ⅓ cup chocolate chips, stirring until smooth.

2. In a medium bowl, combine crushed graham crackers, coconut, and chopped nuts.

3. Stir into butter mixture in saucepan. Mix well and press mixture onto the bottom of an ungreased 10" x 15" jellyroll pan. Refrigerate for 30 minutes, until firm.

4. In a medium mixing bowl, beat softened cream cheese, sugar, and vanilla at medium speed until well blended. Spread mixture over crust. Refrigerate for an additional 30 minutes, until firm.

5. In a separate saucepan over low heat or double boiler, melt remaining ¼ cup butter and remaining ⅔ cup chocolate chips. Once melted, spread mixture over cream cheese layer in pan. Refrigerate until firm before cutting into squares and serving.

Yummy Granola Snack Squares

Ingredients

- 2 ½ cups Rice Krispies cereal
- 2 cups gluten-free oats
- ½ cup raisins
- ½ cup brown sugar
- ½ cup light corn syrup
- ½ cup crunchy peanut butter
- 1 teaspoon vanilla

USE A 9" x 13" PAN

1. In a large bowl, combine Rice Krispies cereal, oats, and raisins. Mix well and set aside.

2. In a small saucepan over medium heat, combine brown sugar and corn syrup. Bring to a boil, remove from heat, and stir in peanut butter and vanilla.

3. Pour mixture over cereal mixture and toss until evenly coated. Press mixture into a greased 9" x 13" baking dish and spread evenly.

4. Let cool to room temperature before cutting into squares and serving.

Peanut Butter Pretzel No-Bakes

USE A 9" x 13" PAN

Ingredients

- ¾ cup margarine, melted
- 1 ½ cups peanut butter
- 1 pound powdered sugar
- 1 (12-ounce) package chocolate chips
- Pretzels, for topping

1. In a large bowl, combine melted margarine, peanut butter, and powdered sugar.

2. Press mixture into the bottom of a greased 9" x 13" pan.

3. In a double boiler, melt chocolate chips. Spread melted chocolate evenly over ingredients in pan. Let cool before cutting into 1-inch squares, topping each one with pretzels. Enjoy!

Holiday Cookies

No matter the holiday, making and eating cookies is a great way to celebrate. The act of making cookies with loved ones creates strong memories that live on year after year. So, whether it's Christmas, Valentine's Day, or Thanksgiving, the cookies in this section will help you celebrate all year-round.

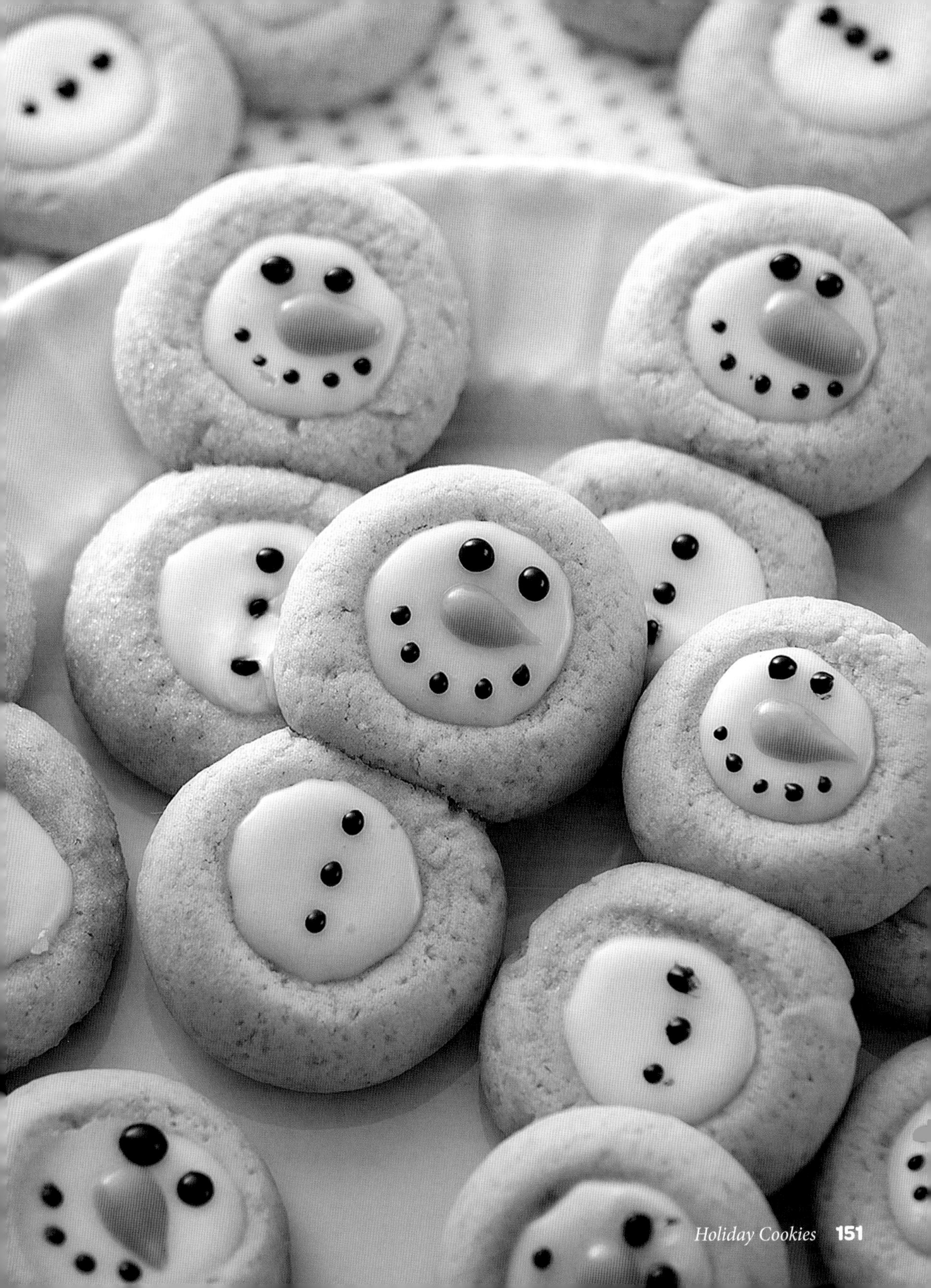

Alphabet Cookie Wishes

MAKES 3 DOZEN

Ingredients

- ½ cup butter, softened
- ½ cup creamy peanut butter
- 1 cup powdered sugar
- ¾ cup brown sugar
- 1 egg
- 1 teaspoon vanilla

- 1 cup flour
- ½ cup unsweetened cocoa powder, plus more for sprinkling
- ¼ teaspoon salt
- Your favorite decorator frosting
- Powdered sugar, for sprinkling, optional

1. In a big bowl, beat butter, peanut butter, powdered sugar, and brown sugar until fluffy. Add egg and vanilla and beat until smooth.

2. In a separate bowl, mix flour, ½ cup cocoa powder, and salt; add to butter mixture a little at a time, stirring until a soft dough forms. Cover and chill several hours or overnight.

3. Preheat your oven to 375°F and line cookie sheets with parchment paper.

4. Put chilled dough on a work surface lightly coated with cocoa powder; sprinkle dough lightly with more cocoa.

5. Roll out dough to ¼-inch thickness and use alphabet cookie cutters (mine were about 2 inches tall) to cut dough into letters to spell out words.

6. Reroll scraps and cut more cookies, chilling dough again as needed. Bake on prepped cookie sheets 7 to 9 minutes or until edges are firm. Transfer to a rack to cool.

7. Pipe on frosting and sprinkle with powdered sugar as desired. Enjoy!

GIFT IDEA

Give a wish spelled out in cookies by lining a gift box with scrapbook paper, creating several dividers. Stack cookie letters on a nest of tissue paper in each section.

Stained Glass Sugar Cookies

MAKES 2 DOZEN

Ingredients

- 1 cup unsalted butter, softened
- ¾ cup sugar
- 1 egg
- 1 teaspoon vanilla
- ¼ teaspoon salt
- 2 ½ cups flour, plus more for rolling
- Small hard candies, crushed (I used red and green Life Savers and blue candy canes)

1. Cream the butter in a mixing bowl on medium speed and gradually beat in the sugar. Beat in the egg, vanilla, and salt until well mixed.

2. Stir in the flour, one-third at a time, until incorporated. Divide the dough in half, flatten, wrap in plastic, and chill overnight.

3. Once the dough is chilled, preheat your oven to 375°F. Line cookie sheets with parchment paper and coat with cooking spray; set aside.

4. Remove one chilled dough portion from the fridge and place on a lightly floured surface; let stand 10 minutes to soften slightly. Lightly flour the dough, cover with a sheet of waxed paper, and roll to ¼-inch thickness.

5. Remove the paper and use a larger cookie cutter to cut shapes from the dough; transfer to the prepped cookie sheets. Remove the centers of the cookies with a smaller cookie cutter. Reroll scraps and repeat.

6. Fill the cut-out part of each cookie with some crushed candy (make sure to get all those nooks and crannies, too) and bake for 10 minutes, until the edges start to brown and the candy is melted.

7. Cool at least 10 minutes, then transfer to cooling racks covered with waxed paper. Repeat with the remaining chilled dough.

8. Store cookies on waxed paper to prevent the candy from sticking. Otherwise, enjoy!

COOKIE ORNAMENT

Poke a small hole in the top of cookies before baking. When cool, attach ribbon and use as a decoration.

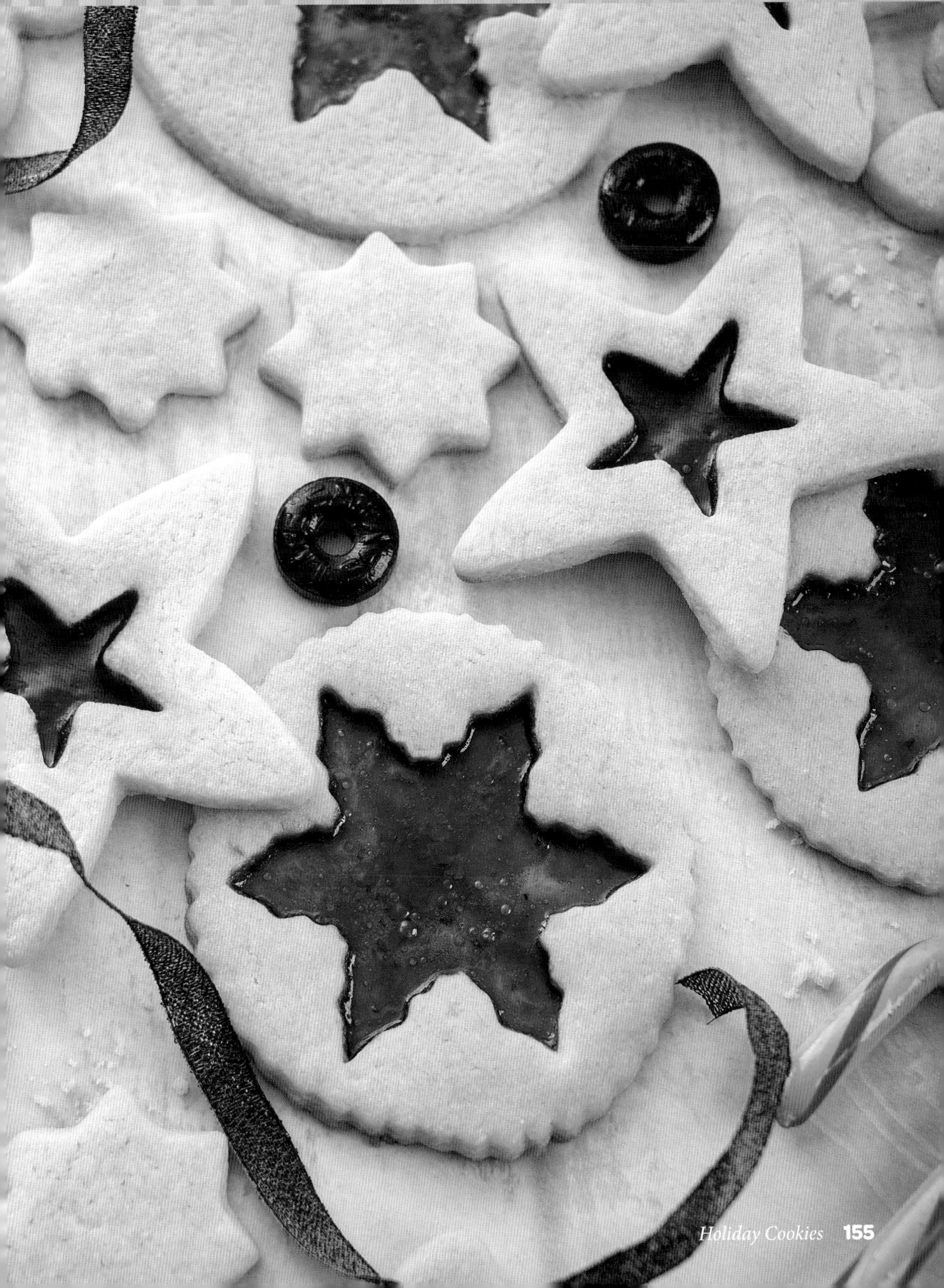

Eggnog Biscotti

MAKES
4
DOZEN

Ingredients

- ½ cup butter, softened
- 1 cup sugar
- 2 eggs
- ½ cup, plus 3 tablespoons purchased eggnog, divided
- 1 ½ teaspoons rum flavoring, divided

- 3 ¼ cups flour, plus more for rolling
- 2 teaspoons baking powder
- 2 teaspoons ground nutmeg
- ½ teaspoon salt
- 1 cup powdered sugar

1. Preheat your oven to 350°F and line a big baking sheet with parchment paper; set aside.

2. For the biscotti, in a big mixing bowl, beat butter, sugar, and eggs until well blended. Mix in eggnog and rum flavoring just until blended.

3. In a separate bowl, stir together flour, baking powder, nutmeg, and salt. Stir the flour mixture into the butter mixture a little at a time until well blended.

4. Divide the dough in half. On a floured surface, shape each half into a 14-inch-long roll and set on the prepped baking sheet, 3 inches apart; flatten slightly. Bake for 25 minutes, until golden brown. Move from the pan to a cooling rack.

5. When cool enough to handle, carefully cut rolls crosswise into ½-inch-thick slices. Place slices cut side down on the baking sheet and bake for 10 minutes. Flip slices over and bake 10 minutes longer, until firm and lightly browned. Transfer to racks set over waxed paper to cool completely.

6. For the glaze, mix the powdered sugar, rum flavoring, and enough eggnog to make a drizzling consistency. Drizzle over the biscotti. Serve and enjoy!

Pecan Snow Drops

MAKES 4 DOZEN

Ingredients

- 2 cups flour
- ¾ teaspoon salt
- 2 cups pecans, chopped, divided
- 1 cup unsalted butter, softened
- ⅓ cup sugar
- 1½ teaspoons vanilla
- Powdered sugar, for dusting

1. Preheat your oven to 325°F and line cookie sheets with parchment paper; set aside.

2. Mix the flour, salt, and 1 cup pecans. Pulse the remaining 1 cup pecans in a food processor until finely ground, then stir them into the flour mixture.

3. In a separate bowl, cream together the butter and sugar. Beat in the vanilla and the flour mixture until incorporated, scraping down the bowl as needed.

4. Roll the dough into scant tablespoon-size balls, arrange on prepped cookie sheets, and bake for 18 minutes or until the bottoms are golden brown. Cool 2 minutes, then move to racks to cool.

5. Roll the cooled cookies in powdered sugar. Let stand 1 hour, then roll in powdered sugar again. Enjoy!

Sugarplums

GLUTEN FREE

Ingredients

- 2 cups almonds
- ¼ cup honey
- 1 ½ teaspoons cinnamon
- ½ teaspoon ground nutmeg
- ¼ teaspoon ground cloves
- 1 ½ cups whole dried apricots
- ½ cup dried plums (prunes)
- ½ cup pitted dates
- Zest of 1 orange
- Pinch of salt
- Powdered sugar, for dusting

MAKES
2 ½
DOZEN

1. Toast the almonds and put in a food processor; pulse until finely chopped.
2. Add all remaining ingredients, pulse until well chopped and beginning to hold together.
3. Roll into balls using a rounded tablespoon for each. Dust with powdered sugar, serve, and enjoy!

Holiday Wreaths

GLUTEN FREE

Ingredients

- 46 large marshmallows
- ½ cup butter
- 1 ½ teaspoons green food coloring
- 3 ½ cups Rice Krispies cereal
- 30 red cinnamon candies

MAKES
10

1. In a large saucepan over low heat, melt marshmallows and butter. Add food coloring and mix until dark green. Gently fold in Rice Krispies.
2. Drop by teaspoonfuls onto waxed paper. Arrange cookies into wreath shapes. Place cinnamon candies on wreaths. Chill in refrigerator until set. Serve end enjoy!

Chocolate-Dipped Cherry Meringues

MAKES 4 DOZEN

GLUTEN FREE
GLUTEN FREE

Ingredients

- 4 egg whites
- ½ teaspoon cream of tartar
- ½ teaspoon salt
- 1 ⅓ cups sugar
- 1 ½ teaspoons cherry flavoring
- Pink paste food coloring, as needed
- ½ cup semi-sweet chocolate chips
- 6 ounces chocolate almond bark

1. Put the egg whites in a big mixing bowl and let stand at room temperature for 30 minutes. Preheat your oven to 225°F and line cookie sheets with parchment paper; set aside.

2. Add cream of tartar and salt to the egg whites and beat on high speed until soft peaks form. Gradually add sugar, 1 tablespoon at a time, beating well after each addition. Continue to beat on high speed until egg whites are glossy and stiff, 5 to 8 minutes. Beat in cherry flavoring and food coloring.

3. Transfer the mixture to a piping bag fitted with the star tip. Pipe 2-inch swirls about 1 inch apart on the prepped cookie sheets. Bake for 1 hour, until dry, firm to the touch, and lightly browned on the bottom. Turn the oven off, keeping the meringues in the oven with the door closed for 1 hour or until cool.

4. In a small microwavable bowl, melt the chocolate chips and almond bark together, stirring until smooth. Carefully dip the bottoms of the cooled meringues into the melted chocolate, allowing the excess to drip off. Set on clean parchment paper until the chocolate is set. Store in an airtight container. Enjoy!

Thumbprint Snow People

MAKES
28

Ingredients

- ½ cup butter, softened
- ¼ cup sugar, plus more for rolling
- ¼ cup brown sugar
- 1 teaspoon baking powder
- ½ teaspoon salt

- 1 egg
- 3 tablespoons milk, divided
- 1 teaspoon vanilla
- 2 cups flour
- 1 ¼ cups powdered sugar, sifted

- ½ teaspoon almond extract
- Orange and black paste food coloring, as needed

1. Preheat your oven to 375°F and line cookie sheets with parchment paper; set aside.

2. In a big bowl, beat butter on medium speed about 30 seconds. Beat in ¼ cup sugar, brown sugar, baking powder, and salt, scraping bowl occasionally. Mix in egg, 1 tablespoon of milk, and vanilla, then beat in the flour until well mixed.

3. For each cookie, shape dough into two ¾-inch balls and place beside each other on the prepped cookie sheets, sides touching.

4. Press a thumb or the back of a small round measuring spoon into each ball to form an indentation. Repeat with remaining dough. (Or make face-only cookies by using one dough ball.)

5. Bake 7 to 9 minutes, until the edges are light brown. Press indentation again. Transfer cookies to a rack to cool.

6. For the icing, stir together the powdered sugar, remaining 2 tablespoons of milk, and almond extract until smooth; fill the cooled cookie indentations with icing and let set several hours to dry.

7. Tint half the remaining icing orange; tint the other half black. When the white icing is dry, decorate the cookies with the colored icing. Serve and enjoy!

Orange-Fennel Roundabouts

MAKES 2 DOZEN

Ingredients

- 1 cup unsalted butter, softened
- ¾ cup sugar
- 1 teaspoon salt
- 2 ½ cups flour, plus more for rolling

- 1 tablespoon fennel seed, crushed to nearly a powder
- 1 ½ tablespoons, plus ½ teaspoon orange zest, divided
- 1 egg, at room temperature

- 1 teaspoon vanilla
- 1 teaspoon orange flavoring
- 2 cups powdered sugar, sifted
- Orange juice, as needed

1. In a mixing bowl, beat the butter, sugar, and salt on high speed for 5 minutes, until fluffy, scraping the bowl often.

2. In a separate bowl, combine 2 ½ cups flour, fennel seed, and 1 ½ tablespoons orange zest.

3. Add the egg, vanilla, and orange flavoring, stirring until combined; add to the butter mixture and beat on low speed until just combined. Form the dough into two disks, wrap in plastic, and chill at least an hour.

4. Preheat your oven to 350°F and line cookie sheets with parchment paper; spritz the paper with cooking spray. Set aside.

5. Let one dough disk stand at room temperature a few minutes to soften. On a lightly floured surface, roll out the dough about ¼ inch thick and cut out 3-inch rounds; set on prepped cookie sheets, 1 inch apart. Bake 13 to 15 minutes or until just golden around the edges. Transfer to a cooling rack set over waxed paper. Repeat with remaining dough.

6. For the frosting, whisk together the powdered sugar, ½ teaspoon orange zest, and enough orange juice to make spreading consistency; frost the cooled cookies. Sprinkle with more zest if you'd like. Enjoy!

Peppermint Dips

MAKES 3 DOZEN

Ingredients

- 1 cup flour
- ½ cup unsweetened cocoa powder, plus more for rolling
- ½ teaspoon baking soda
- ½ teaspoon baking powder
- ½ teaspoon salt
- 5 tablespoons unsalted butter, softened
- ¾ cup sugar
- 1 egg plus 1 egg yolk
- ¾ teaspoon peppermint extract
- 1¼ pounds white or chocolate almond bark, coarsely chopped
- 15 round peppermint candies, crushed

1. Sift the flour, ½ cup cocoa powder, baking soda, baking powder, and salt into a bowl.

2. In a mixing bowl, beat butter and sugar on medium-high speed for 1 minute; reduce speed to medium-low and add egg, then egg yolk, beating well after each addition. Beat in peppermint extract.

3. Slowly beat in the flour mixture until just incorporated. Shape into two flat disks, wrap in plastic, and refrigerate at least 1 hour.

4. Working with one portion at a time, lightly coat both sides of dough with cocoa powder and roll between two pieces of parchment paper to ⅛-inch thickness; chill for 15 minutes.

5. Preheat your oven to 325°F. Cut 2-inch circles from dough and arrange on parchment paper–lined baking sheets. Roll and cut scraps once. Freeze cookies for 15 minutes.

6. Bake for 12 minutes or until cookies are dry to the touch. Transfer to racks to cool. Let the baking sheets cool and line with clean parchment paper.

7. Melt the almond bark in a double boiler over low heat. Using a fork, dip each cookie into the melted bark to coat, letting excess drip off; gently scrape the bottom against the edge of the pan.

8. Set on prepped baking sheets and sprinkle with candy. Repeat with the remaining cookies. Let dry. Enjoy!

PACKAGE THEM!

Cut pretty paper to fit inside a cellophane bag and tuck in some cookies.
Add a paper topper and a ribbon for a gift that's sure to please.

Holiday Swirls

MAKES
2
DOZEN

Ingredients

- ⅔ cup shortening
- ⅔ cup butter
- 1½ cups sugar
- 2 eggs, lightly beaten
- 3½ cups flour
- 1 teaspoon salt
- 2 teaspoons baking powder
- 2 teaspoons vanilla
- Red and green paste food coloring, as needed
- Decorating sprinkles, as needed

1. In a mixing bowl, beat shortening, butter, sugar, and eggs. Beat in the flour, salt, baking powder, and vanilla on low speed until incorporated. Increase speed to medium and beat until well blended.

2. Divide the dough into three separate bowls. Mix red food coloring into one bowl—you'll need quite a bit to get a deep, rich color. Do the same to another bowl using green. Keep the third bowl plain.

3. Roll out each color on separate pieces of waxed paper to about ⅛-inch thickness, making them all about the same size. Carefully flip one on top of the other, lining up edges of dough as much as possible and removing the waxed paper after flipping. Once stacked, use a pizza cutter to trim edges straight.

4. Starting at one long side, roll the layers tightly together, lifting up the waxed paper underneath to help roll. Wrap the waxed paper around the roll and chill overnight.

5. Preheat your oven to 375°F. Use a sharp knife to cut dough into ⅝-inch-thick slices. Roll the edges in decorating sprinkles and set on a parchment paper–lined cookie sheet. Bake about 10 minutes, until just barely done. Serve and enjoy!

Holly Jolly Pretzel Bites

MAKES 3 DOZEN

Ingredients

- 1 cup flour
- ⅓ cup unsweetened cocoa powder
- ¼ teaspoon salt
- ½ cup unsalted butter, softened
- ⅓ cup sugar

- ⅓ cup light brown sugar
- 1 egg yolk
- 1 ½ teaspoons vanilla
- 2 tablespoons buttermilk
- 1 cup pretzels, finely chopped

- 15 caramels, unwrapped
- 2 ½ tablespoons heavy cream
- Coarse sea salt, to taste
- ½ cup milk chocolate chips
- 1 teaspoon vegetable oil

1. In a bowl, mix flour, cocoa powder, and salt.

2. In a big mixing bowl, beat butter, sugar, and brown sugar until pale and fluffy.

3. Mix in egg yolk and vanilla. Blend in the buttermilk. Slowly add the flour mixture, beating on low speed until just incorporated. Cover dough and chill at least an hour.

4. Preheat your oven to 350°F and line cookie sheets with parchment paper. Shape the chilled dough into 1-inch balls and roll in the pretzels to coat. Arrange on prepped baking sheets and use your thumb to make a deep indentation in the center of each. Bake 10 to 12 minutes.

5. Remove the cookies from the oven and use a rounded measuring spoon to press down on the existing indentation. Cool several minutes before moving to a rack to cool.

6. For the filling, combine caramels and cream in a glass bowl and microwave until melted and smooth, stirring every 30 seconds. Spoon caramel into the cookies' indentations; sprinkle with sea salt.

7. Melt chocolate chips with oil in the microwave at 50% power. Transfer to a small, zippered plastic bag; zip shut, cut off a tiny corner, and drizzle chocolate over cookies. Let stand until cool. Enjoy!

Nutcracker Peanut Blossoms

MAKES 6 DOZEN

Ingredients

- 1 cup shortening
- 1 cup creamy peanut butter
- 1 cup brown sugar
- 1 cup sugar, plus more for rolling
- 2 eggs
- ¼ cup, plus 2 tablespoons milk, divided
- 2 ½ teaspoons vanilla, divided
- 3 ½ cups flour
- 2 teaspoons baking soda
- 1 teaspoon salt
- ½ cup butter, softened
- 2 ½ cups powdered sugar
- ½ cup unsweetened cocoa powder, sifted
- 2 tablespoons light corn syrup

1. Preheat your oven to 375°F and grease cookie sheets; set aside.

2. Cream together the shortening, peanut butter, brown sugar, and 1 cup sugar until smooth. Beat in the eggs one at a time; stir in ¼ cup milk and 2 teaspoons vanilla.

3. In a separate bowl, mix the flour, baking soda, and salt; stir into the peanut butter mixture until well blended. Shape tablespoonfuls of dough into balls and roll in more sugar.

4. Arrange 2 inches apart on prepped cookie sheets. Bake 12 to 14 minutes, until golden brown and cracked.

5. Remove from the oven and immediately use a rounded measuring spoon to gently press an indentation into the center of the cookies. Transfer to a rack to cool.

6. For the frosting, mix the butter and ½ teaspoon vanilla. Slowly beat in the powdered sugar and cocoa powder; stir in 2 tablespoons milk and corn syrup.

7. Beat on high speed to desired consistency and transfer the mixture to a piping bag fitted with a star tip; pipe into the center of the cooled cookies. Serve and enjoy!

Lemon Tartlets

MAKES 1½ DOZEN

Ingredients

- ½ cup butter, softened
- ½ cup sugar, plus more for tossing
- 1 egg
- ¾ teaspoon lemon flavoring
- ¾ teaspoons vanilla, divided
- 2 teaspoons lemon zest
- 1 ½ cups flour
- ⅛ teaspoon salt
- ½ cup heavy cream
- 3 tablespoons powdered sugar
- 1 (10-ounce) jar lemon curd
- ½ cup sour cream
- ½ teaspoon vanilla
- 1 lemon, for topping
- Whipped cream, for topping
- Fresh berries, for topping

1. Preheat your oven to 375°F. For the shells, cream the butter, then beat in sugar until well blended. Mix in the egg, lemon flavoring, vanilla, and lemon zest. Add the flour and salt, mixing to make a stiff dough; chill at least 2 hours.

2. Roll dough into 1¼-inch balls and press one into a thin even layer over the bottom and up the side of the tart tins. Bake about 10 minutes, until edges start to brown. Set tins upside down and when cool enough to handle, pinch edges slightly to remove the shells; cool completely.

3. For the filling, beat the cream with powdered sugar until stiff peaks form. In a separate bowl, whisk together lemon curd, sour cream, and vanilla; fold in the prepped whipped cream. Spoon into cool shells and freeze at least 4 hours.

4. Just before serving, peel thin strips of rind from the lemon and toss with sugar. Remove tartlets from freezer and top with whipped cream, berries, and lemon strips. Enjoy!

Candy Cane Twists

Flavored with peppermint, these old-time cookies will bring smiles to young and old alike.

MAKES 2 ½ DOZEN

Ingredients

- ½ cup shortening
- ½ cup butter, softened
- 1 cup powdered sugar, plus more for sprinkling
- 1 egg
- 1 ½ teaspoons peppermint extract, as needed
- 1 teaspoon vanilla
- 2 ½ cups flour, plus more for rolling
- ¾ teaspoon salt
- Red food coloring, as needed

1. Preheat your oven to 375°F and line cookie sheets with parchment paper.

2. Beat together the shortening, butter, and powdered sugar just until well combined. Add the egg, peppermint extract, and vanilla and mix well. Stir in 2 ½ cups flour and salt.

3. Transfer half the dough to another bowl and stir in food coloring until well blended. Chill both bowls for 15 minutes.

4. On a lightly floured surface, roll about ½ tablespoon red dough into a 1-inch ball and then roll it into a rope about 5 inches long; do the same with the plain dough. Lay the ropes side by side and twist together.

5. Set on prepped cookie sheets and curve the top to look like a candy cane. Repeat with the remaining dough. Bake for 6 to 9 minutes, until cookies are set and are just barely turning golden brown underneath.

6. Let cookies cool on the pan for a minute or two before removing to a rack to cool completely. Sprinkle with a little powdered sugar. Serve and enjoy!

Fudgy Elf Bites

GLUTEN FREE

MAKES 50

Ingredients

- 3 cups semi-sweet chocolate chips
- 1 (14-ounce) can sweetened condensed milk
- 2 tablespoons, plus ¾ cup unsalted butter, divided
- 1 teaspoon vanilla
- 1 cup chopped walnuts
- 2 cups sugar

- ¾ cup heavy cream
- Pinch of salt
- 2 cups white baking chips
- 1 (7-ounce) jar marshmallow crème
- 2 tablespoons dry strawberry gelatin

1. Melt the chocolate chips with the condensed milk and 2 tablespoons of butter. Stir in the vanilla and walnuts. Spread evenly into a 9" x 9" foil-lined and greased pan.

2. Boil together ¾ cup of butter, the sugar, heavy cream, and salt for 5 minutes, stirring constantly; remove from heat.

3. Use a hand mixer to beat in the white baking chips and marshmallow crème until smooth; pour half over the chocolate layer. To the remainder, beat in the dry strawberry gelatin; drop by spoonfuls into pan and swirl gently with a knife.

4. Chill before cutting. Serve and enjoy! (You can't have just one!)

Cream Cheese Spritz

MAKES 8 DOZEN

Ingredients

- 2 cups butter, softened
- 1 (8-ounce) package cream cheese, softened
- 1 cup plus 3 tablespoons sugar
- 2 teaspoons vanilla
- 4 ½ cups sifted flour

- Paste food coloring, optional
- Colored sugars and/or decorating sprinkles, optional
- Almond bark or candy melts, any color, optional

1. Preheat your oven to 375°F and chill your cookie sheets.

2. In a mixing bowl, cream together the butter and cream cheese until smooth. Add sugar and beat until well combined. Beat in vanilla and slowly add the flour, beating until well mixed. Stir in the food coloring if you're using it.

3. Transfer the dough to a cookie press fitted with the desired decorating plate. Form cookies on an ungreased chilled cookie sheet by setting the end of the cookie press against the cookie sheet and pressing out the shapes you want.

4. Decorate cookies with colored sugars or decorating sprinkles now if you're not going to coat them in almond bark later.

5. Bake 8 to 10 minutes, until lightly browned underneath. Move to a rack to cool.

6. For coated cookies, after baking, melt almond bark or candy melts in a small bowl in the microwave at 50% power, stirring until smooth.

7. Set a cooled cookie on a fork above the bowl while drizzling the bark over the top and sides of the cookie; tap the fork against bowl to remove excess and set on a rack over waxed paper. Decorate with sugars or sprinkles.

8. Repeat with remaining cookies. Let stand until the coating is dry. Enjoy

COOKIE PLATE, ANYONE?

Using enamel acrylic paint (for glass and ceramics), paint a design on a white ceramic plate; set on a baking sheet and place in a cold oven. Set oven temperature to 300°F and heat the plate for 30 minutes, then set aside to cool. Now just pile on the cookies!

Whether you color them, dip them, or eat them straight-up plain, these cookies practically scream nostalgia!

Gingerbread Village Centerpiece

Ingredients

- ½ cup plus 1 tablespoon butter
- ½ cup brown sugar
- ½ cup light corn syrup
- 2 teaspoons ground ginger
- ½ teaspoon cinnamon

- 1 teaspoon ground nutmeg
- ½ teaspoon ground cloves
- 2 ½ cups flour, sifted
- 1 teaspoon baking soda
- Powdered sugar, as needed

- Frosting and decorating sprinkles, optional
- Sugar, for plating

1. In a mixing bowl, cream together the butter and brown sugar until fluffy. Add the syrup, ginger, cinnamon, nutmeg, and cloves.

2. In a separate bowl, mix the flour and baking soda and add it to the butter mixture, beating until well blended. Divide dough in half, flatten into disks, and wrap in plastic; chill until firm.

3. Let one disk soften slightly, then roll it out ³⁄₁₆ inch thick between sheets of parchment paper. Cut house and tree shapes using cookie cutters (ours were about 4 to 7 inches tall) or cut out free-hand. Press details like shingles and doors into the dough using a knife or toothpick. Slide parchment and cookies onto a tray and chill 15 to 20 minutes.

4. Preheat your oven to 375°F. Transfer parchment and cookies to cookie sheets. Bake 8 to 10 minutes, until done. Transfer to racks to cool. Roll, cut, and bake remaining chilled dough.

5. Sprinkle powdered sugar liberally over cooled cookies and gently rub in. Cover with waxed paper and let stand 30 minutes. Decorate with frosting and sprinkles if you'd like. Fill the bowl with a few inches of sugar and arrange the cookies in the sugar. Enjoy!

DON'T FORGET THE GINGERBREAD MAN!

Use a gingerbread-man-shaped cookie cutter when you're on step 3 to make a classic Christmastime pal to go with your centerpiece! For the decorative icing, just combine 1 ¼ cups powdered sugar, ½ teaspoon vanilla extract, 2 tablespoons milk, and food coloring of your choice. Put in a piping bag and decorate away!

Peppermint Cookie Bark

USE A 9" x 13" PAN

Ingredients

- ½ cup butter, softened
- 1 cup sugar
- 1 egg
- ¼ to ½ teaspoon peppermint extract
- 2 whole graham cracker rectangles, crushed
- 1 ½ cups flour
- ½ teaspoon baking powder
- ¼ teaspoon salt

- 1 (12-ounce) package semisweet chocolate chips
- 1 ¼ cups white baking chips, divided
- 1 teaspoon shortening
- ¼ cup dark chocolate chips
- About ½ cup red-striped hard candies or candy canes, coarsely crushed

1. Preheat the oven to 350°F. Grease or line a 9" x 13" baking pan and set aside. In a mixing bowl, beat the butter and sugar until light and fluffy. Beat in the egg and peppermint extract until well blended.

2. In a separate bowl, whisk together the cracker crumbs, flour, baking powder, and salt and add slowly to the creamed mixture, stirring until combined. Press evenly into the prepped pan and bake for 22 to 25 minutes, until golden brown. Immediately sprinkle the semisweet chocolate chips over the top.

3. Return to the oven for a minute or two until softened then spread evenly. Cool in the pan on a wire rack then chill until the chocolate has hardened.

4. Melt 1 cup of the white baking chips with the shortening; stir to combine, set aside for 10 minutes, and spread over the hardened chocolate layer, nearly to the edges.

5. In separate bowls, melt the remaining ¼ cup white baking chips and the dark chocolate chips; drizzle both over the white layer. Immediately sprinkle the crushed candy over the top before cutting into bars. Enjoy!

Double-Decker Almond Bars

USE A 9"x13" PAN

Ingredients

- 1 ½ cups butter, softened, divided
- 2 cups sugar
- 4 eggs
- 3 teaspoons almond extract, divided
- 5 cups flour

- 1 teaspoon, plus 1 pinch salt, divided
- ½ teaspoon baking soda
- Green and red food coloring (or colors of your choice)
- 4 cups powdered sugar, sifted

- 5 tablespoons milk
- 1 teaspoon almond extract
- Sliced almonds, for topping

1. Preheat the oven to 375°F. Grease or line a 9" x 13" baking pan and set aside. In a mixing bowl, cream together 1 cup butter and the sugar until light and fluffy. Beat in eggs, one at a time, until combined then mix in 2 teaspoons almond extract.

2. In a separate bowl, sift together the flour, 1 teaspoon salt, and baking soda and slowly mix into the creamed mixture, until just combined. Divide the batter among two small bowls. Stir green food coloring into one bowl and red food coloring into the other. Spread dough into prepped pan, layering one color over the other. Bake for 25 to 30 minutes until it tests done with a toothpick. Set the pan on a wire rack to cool completely.

3. For the frosting, in a mixing bowl, cream together the powdered sugar, a pinch of salt, ½ cup butter, milk, and 1 teaspoon almond extract until smooth and stiff. Spread over cooled cookie, cut into bars, and arrange almonds on top. Enjoy!

These make a great treat for a holiday because you can match your food coloring to the occasion!

Cozy Almond Toffee

SERVES A CROWD

Ingredients

- 1 ¼ cups almonds, coarsely chopped, divided
- 1 cup unsalted butter, cubed
- 1 cup sugar
- ½ teaspoon vanilla
- ¼ teaspoon salt
- 1 ½ cups mini semi-sweet chocolate chips

1. Toast almonds; set aside ¼ cup and put the remainder in a single layer in a 9" x 13" pan lined with parchment paper.

2. In a saucepan over medium heat, heat the butter sugar, vanilla, and salt 10 to 15 minutes, until caramel-colored, whisking constantly; drizzle evenly over the almonds in the pan and sprinkle with the chocolate chips.

3. When the chips have softened, spread evenly and sprinkle with the set-aside almonds. When cool, break into pieces and serve!

Oatmeal Pumpkin Bars

Ingredients

- 2 cups gluten-free old-fashioned oats
- ½ cup pumpkin puree
- 2 tablespoons maple syrup
- ⅓ cup coconut oil, melted
- ¼ cup coconut sugar
- 2 teaspoons vanilla
- 1 teaspoon baking powder
- ½ teaspoon cinnamon
- ½ teaspoon salt
- ¾ cup white baking chips, divided

USE AN 8" x 8" PAN

1. Preheat the oven to 325°F and grease or line an 8" x 8" baking pan; set aside.

2. In a high-speed blender or food processor, blend the oats until the texture of flour. Add the pumpkin puree, maple syrup, oil, sugar, vanilla, baking powder, cinnamon, and salt and process until smooth.

3. Transfer the mixture to a bowl and stir in ½ cup of the baking chips. Press the dough into the prepped pan, sprinkle with the remaining ¼ cup baking chips, and bake for 25 minutes (they will appear underbaked). Cool in the pan on a wire rack then chill about an hour before cutting into bars. Enjoy!

Harvest Cookies

USE A
10"x15"
PAN

Ingredients

- ½ cup softened butter
- 1 (16- to 18-ounce) package yellow cake mix
- 1 egg
- 3 ½ cups mini marshmallows
- ½ cup light corn syrup
- ¼ cup sugar
- ¼ cup brown sugar
- ½ cup creamy peanut butter
- 2 teaspoons vanilla
- 2 ½ cups Crispex cereal
- 1 ½ cups dry roasted peanuts
- 1 cup candy corn

1. Preheat the oven to 350°F. Beat together the butter, cake mix, and egg until it holds together; press into an ungreased 10" x 15" baking pan and bake for 15 minutes or until the edges are golden brown.

2. Put the mini marshmallows in a single layer over the cookie. Bake for 2 minutes more to puff the marshmallows; set aside.

3. In a saucepan over medium heat, combine the corn syrup, sugar, and brown sugar and heat until boiling, stirring often.

4. Remove from the heat and stir in the peanut butter and vanilla until well mixed. Stir in the Crispex, peanuts, and candy corn until coated.

5. Drop mounds of the mixture over the marshmallows and spread gently. Cool before cutting into bars and gobbling up!

Pumpkin Cheesecake Doodles

MAKES
2 ½
DOZEN

Ingredients

- 3 ¾ cups flour
- 1 ½ teaspoon baking powder
- ½ teaspoon salt
- ¼ teaspoon ground nutmeg
- 2 ½ teaspoons cinnamon, divided

- 1 cup unsalted butter, softened
- ½ cup brown sugar
- 1 ¾ cups sugar, divided
- 1 cup pumpkin puree
- 1 egg

- 4 teaspoons vanilla, divided
- 1 (8-ounce) package cream cheese, softened
- 1 teaspoon ground ginger
- ⅛ teaspoon ground allspice

1. Whisk together the flour, baking powder, salt, nutmeg, and ½ teaspoon cinnamon in a bowl and set aside.

2. In a mixing bowl, beat together the butter, brown sugar, and 1 cup sugar on medium speed until fluffy, 2 to 3 minutes. Beat in the pumpkin puree, egg, and 2 teaspoons vanilla. Slowly beat in the set-aside flour mixture until just combined. Cover and chill dough for 1 hour.

3. For the filling, beat together the cream cheese, ¼ cup sugar, and remaining 2 teaspoons vanilla until blended; cover and chill for 1 hour.

4. For the sugar coating, mix the ginger, allspice, and the remaining 2 teaspoons cinnamon and 1 cup sugar in a small bowl; set aside.

5. To bake the cookies, preheat the oven to 350°F and line cookie sheets with parchment paper. Set 1 tablespoon dough into the set-aside sugar coating; flatten dough slightly and turn to coat the other side.

6. Set dough on a prepped cookie sheet and top with 1 teaspoon filling. Coat another tablespoonful of dough in the same way and place it over the filling; pinch edges to seal the sweet creamy filling inside, then gently roll into a ball. Roll in sugar coating and return to the cookie sheet. Repeat, spacing cookies 2 inches apart. (Keep any remaining cookie dough and filling chilled between batches.)

7. Bake 15 to 20 minutes or until tops start to crack. Let cool 5 minutes before removing to a wire rack to finish cooling. Store in the refrigerator. Enjoy!

Cheesecake: delicious.
Snickerdoodles: yummy. Pumpkin
pie: divine. Putting cheesecake
inside a pumpkin-flavored
doodle: GENIUS!

Love Potion Crispy Bites

USE A
9" x 13"
PAN

GLUTEN FREE

Ingredients

- 3 tablespoons butter or margarine
- 1 (10.5-ounce) package miniature marshmallows
- 2 teaspoons cherry extract
- 1 teaspoon red food coloring
- 6 cups Rice Krispies cereal

1. In a large saucepan over low heat, melt butter. Add marshmallows and stir until completely melted. Remove from heat.

2. Stir in cherry extract and red food coloring. Add Rice Krispies cereal, stirring until completely coated.

3. Using a greased spatula, press mixture evenly into a greased 9" x 13" pan. Let cool. Use a heart-shaped cookie cutter to cut individual treats. Enjoy!

Red Hot Divinity Bars

GLUTEN FREE

MAKES
8

Ingredients

- 2 egg whites
- ¼ teaspoon cream of tartar
- 2 ½ cups sugar
- ½ cup light corn syrup
- ½ cup hot water
- ¼ teaspoon salt
- ½ cup Red Hots candies
- 1 teaspoon vanilla

1. In the bowl of a stand mixer, beat the egg whites until foamy; add the cream of tartar and beat until stiff peaks form. Butter a 5" x 9" loaf pan; set aside.

2. In a heavy saucepan over medium heat, mix the sugar, corn syrup, hot water, salt, and Red Hots until boiling, stirring constantly; cover and boil 3 minutes undisturbed.

3. Uncover, attach a candy thermometer, and heat to 260°F without stirring; pour into the egg whites in a slow, steady stream, beating constantly. Add vanilla and beat until stiff peaks form. Immediately spread into prepped pan. Cool, then cut into squares. Enjoy!

No-Bake Easter Nests

MAKES 6

Ingredients

- 3 tablespoons butter or margarine
- 3 cups miniature marshmallows
- 4 cups chow mein noodles
- Small jelly beans, M&Ms, or other small candies, for topping

1. Line a baking sheet with waxed paper.

2. In a large saucepan, melt butter and marshmallows over medium heat, stirring until smooth.

3. In a large bowl, combine chow mein noodles and melted marshmallow mixture. Stir until noodles are well coated.

4. Roll mixture into 6 round balls. Place balls on prepared baking sheet.

5. With the back of a teaspoon, press center of each ball to make an indentation. Let nests set until firm.

6. Fill each nest with small jelly beans or other small candies like M&Ms, gumdrops, or chocolate-covered peanuts.

Index

Note: Page numbers in **bold** indicate lists of recipes by cookie category. Asterisks (*) after recipe titles indicate Gluten-Free recipes.